# Sites of Multilingualism:
## Complementary Schools in Britain Today

# Sites of Multilingualism:
## Complementary Schools in Britain Today

*Edited by Vally Lytra and Peter Martin*

**Trentham Books**
Stoke on Trent, UK and Sterling, USA

Trentham Books Limited
Westview House    22883 Quicksilver Drive
734 London Road   Sterling
Oakhill            VA 20166-2012
Stoke on Trent     USA
Staffordshire
England ST4 5NP

First published 2010

British Library Cataloguing-in-Publication Data
A catalogue record for this book is available from the British Library

ISBN: 978-1-85856-454-8

Designed and typeset by Trentham Books Ltd, Stoke-on-Trent and printed in Great Britain by Page Bros (Norwich) Ltd, Norfolk.

# Contents

*To our dear friend and colleague Peter Martin,*
*whose passion for bilingualism and complementary schooling,*
*and his kindness and generosity touched so many of us*

# Peter Martin – notes of appreciation

I met Peter only a few times at conferences, but we worked together on many projects, including his co-edited book on *Multilingual Classroom Ecologies* (2003) and the *Encyclopedia of Language and Education* volume on *Ecology of Language* (2008) which he co-edited with Angela Creese and me. His research on multilingual education and language policy – whether in classrooms of Brunei or complementary schools in England – consistently offers both ethnographic depth and theoretical purchase. I have found his work full of insight and have shared it often with my students. Though we have lost him too soon, he will be remembered with much fondness and appreciation. He was a dedicated scholar, deep thinker, and kind human being.

*Nancy Hornberger, University of Pennsylvania, U.S.A.*


While based in our own national and regional contexts, we are sometime fortunate to meet an exceptional colleague, who has had a wealth of local and international experience that helps to inform our own research efforts and practice. Peter Martin was such a colleague. I first met Peter at a session of the American Association for Applied Linguistics, at which he and colleagues presented on multilingualism in the UK. The implications of their research efforts in the UK for ours were apparent and energising. Peter's direct research connections with multilingual schools and communities have provided a model for connecting theory and practice. His more recent efforts on supplemental education in the UK have been equally relevant. He will be greatly missed, but his work will continue to inspire and energise.

*Terrence G. Wiley, Arizona State University, U.S.A.*

Although I never met Peter Martin personally, I have been heavily influenced by his writings on multilingualism in education and his commitment to the education of language minority students. Through his work I have been able to understand aspects of classroom teaching and bilingual interaction that have deeply impacted my own work. Peter Martin's scholarship integrated fields of thinking and contributed new ways of understanding bilingualism. His recent research on complementary schools in Britain has been promising and exciting, and I have followed it with curiosity and awe since its inception. The recent issue of the *Journal of Bilingual Education and Bilingualism*, co-edited by Peter Martin and Li Wei, looked at code-switching in the classroom in new ways. The volume reminded me of my own work on translanguaging. As I started to raise questions, I realised that many would have to be un-answered because of his absence. The void he leaves is deeply felt. It is only fortunate that he has closely collaborated with colleagues like Vally Lytra who will continue to build on his work to develop further understandings of multilingualism in schools for the future. I am grateful for all he has taught me through his work.

*Ofelia García, Graduate Center, City University of New York, U.S.A.*

As Peter's publisher, I came to know him in a particular way. In this book and in *Multilingual Learning – stories from schools and communities in Britain* Peter was co-editor, here with Vally and in the earlier volume with Jean and Leena (who both contribute to the volume in your hands). When they introduced him to me I was struck by his modesty, which sat comfortably with his total command of the research he was presenting at that year's BERA in Wales. It was the crisis of Jean's illness that led to my working directly with him on the earlier book. What I call the endgame can be demanding and I was impressed with how Peter stepped up and, with quiet thoroughness, saw it through to publication.

When he approached me about the present collection, with Vally as co-editor, I didn't hesitate: I knew it would be rigorous, coherent and that I could rely on their professionalism. Now it is Vally who has stepped up. We can all be grateful to her for seeing this fine book through to its final form as a fitting tribute to Peter Martin: a fine scholar, a highly professional author and editor and a lovely man.

*Gillian Klein, Editorial Director of Trentham Books*

# Introduction

## *Vally Lytra and Peter Martin*

This volume is motivated by the increasing acceptance of the linguistic, cultural and social significance of complementary schools in the lives and experiences of new arrivals and ethnic minority children, their families and communities in Britain today. Although complementary schooling is still an under-researched area, there is now a critical mass of recent and on-going language-focused research on complementary schools among ethno-linguistic communities, some of them settled and others recently arrived. The aims of this book are to bring together this body of research to explore aspects of:

- language and literacy practices
- the negotiation of social identities and affiliations
- policy and practice

The book also suggests theoretical frameworks and research methodologies which enable us to understand interaction, learning and identity formation processes in these schools.

Complementary schools are voluntary schools, also referred to as community, supplementary or Saturday schools. They are set up by specific linguistic, cultural or religious communities for a range of functions, particularly the maintenance of community languages and cultures for fear that these might be lost over the generations. Following Creese and Martin (2006), we use the term complementary schools in order to highlight 'the positive complementary function between these schools and mainstream schools for those who teach and learn in them' (p1). Defining these schools as complementary also stresses their importance in the lives of the children, their families and communities more generally and 'their contribution to political, social and economic life in the wider community' (*ibid*). Although we recognise that language terminology is ideologically-laden, we choose not to be prescriptive about the choice of terms. While the term 'complementary schools' is used in the title of this book and in many of its chapters, contributing authors have also used the terms 'community language and culture classes', 'community schools' or 'community language and culture schools'. All terms share an understanding of complementary schools as sites for learning, socialising and play where bilingualism/multilingualism is the norm and where interaction is usually characterised by simultaneous and flexible language use. Moreover, they share an understanding of the role the schools play not only in complementing the young people's mainstream school educational experience but also in providing them with spaces to develop and transform aspects of their multilingual repertoires and identities that often go unrecognised in mainstream schools and society at large.

The lack of recognition of the experiences of young people, their families and communities and their language, cultural and religious expressions as well as concerns about children's underachievement in mainstream schools and society prompted communities to set up complementary schools. Some complementary schools were set up as early as the19th century but the bulk of schools were organised from the late 1960s onwards. In his historical overview of complementary schooling in the UK, Li Wei (2006) identifies three broad groups of complementary schools that emerged from that time.

The first group targeted children of African-Caribbean families who were concerned by widespread perceptions of their children's underachievement and the racism and overt prejudice they faced. The second group came about in the late 1970s and early 1980s, when Muslim, Sikh and Hindu communities of South Asian and African origins wanted separate, religious schools for their children and where Arabic was taught alongside community languages. The third group were organised at around the same period by other immigrant and ethnic minority communities wishing to maintain their heritage language and culture (p76-78).

This book reports on research from the second and mainly third group of schools (but see Issa and Williams 2009 for an extensive treatment of black schools in the UK). Although the specific socio-historical context for the emergence and development of the different groups of complementary schools and their main concerns may have differed, one common feature was that they provided a response by communities to the failure of the mainstream education system to meet the needs of new arrivals and ethnic minority children (Li Wei, 2006:78). In the context of ongoing public debates over language diversity and multiculturalism, complementary schools present a challenge to the predominantly monolingual and unicultural ideologies of mainstream education and society. In so doing, they play a central role in wider debate about language and educational practices and policies in British society today (Creese and Martin, 2006; Conteh *et al*, 2007b).

## The structure of this book

Chapters are clustered around three broad themes: language and literacy practices, identity processes and practice and policy. Importantly however, themes cut across and mutually inform chapters. In the ensuing sections, we discuss some key issues around these themes and provide brief overviews of each chapter. Although each chapter describes a particular community or communities, we acknowledge that communities themselves are heterogeneous and diverse entities that are subject to change over time.

Similar to the communities described, the chapters themselves are heterogeneous in style: some are written in academic prose and others read like stories. This divergence of style reflects the different voices and experiences of the young people, parents, teachers and other school staff as well as those of the contributors across complementary school settings in Britain. The book has coherence overall, however, for two reasons. It illustrates shared theoretical and methodological concerns, and the chapters are systematically cross-referenced.

### *Language and literacy practices*

Complementary schools are multilingual and multiliterate sites which provide a safe space outside mainstream schools for the maintenance and transformation of young people's community languages and cultures (eg Creese and Martin, 2006; Gregory, 1993; Gregory *et al*, 2004; Li Wei, 2006). A number of studies have documented the rich and complex language ecologies in complementary schools and classrooms (eg Arthur, 2003; Martin *et al*, 2004; Kenner, 2004; Kenner *et al*, 2007, also Lytra *et al*, Ruby *et al* and Sneddon, all in this volume). At the same time, they have identified generational differences in beliefs and practices of language use among young people, parents, teachers and other staff (eg Gregory and Williams 2000; Kenner *et al*, 2004; Li Wei, 1994). Moreover, they have identified linguistic hierarchies between languages as well as standard forms of the community language and its language varieties and divergent views about the teaching of heritage, history and culture in complementary schools (Creese *et al*, 2008, also Blackledge and Creese, Li Wei and Chao-Jung Wu, all in this volume).

A shared theoretical starting point for these studies as well as the chapters in this book is an understanding of language and literacy practices as socially and politically constructed. This is premised on a view of bilingualism/multilingualism that, as Heller (2007) argues, moves away 'from a focus on whole bounded units of code and community, and towards a more processual and materialistic approach which privileges language as social practice, speakers as social actors and boundaries as products of social action' (p1). The shift of focus from code to social actors provides a useful perspective to examine the ways children, teachers and parents draw on sets of linguistic resources for learning, socialising and play. These linguistic resources 'circulate in unequal ways in social networks and discursive spaces, whose meaning and values are socially constructed within the constraints of social organisational processes, under specific historical conditions' (Heller, 2007:2). This view of language illuminates the interrelationship between agency and social structure and draws connections across micro (interactional), meso (institutional) and macro (wider socio-political) levels of analysis.

The first three chapters are drawn from two linked ESRC-funded project which looked at the multilingual practices and identity performances of young people and their teachers (Creese *et al*, 2008; Martin *et al*, 2004).

In Chapter One, *Opening up flexible spaces: ideology and practice in complementary schools,* Adrian Blackledge and Angela Creese draw on interactional data from a range of settings (eg classroom, home and Qur'anic Arabic tutoring sessions) and interviews with young people, parents and staff in Bengali schools to trace two seemingly contradictory language ideologies in heritage language teaching and learning in complementary schools. They illustrate how complementary schools open up spaces in which young people and their teachers can juxtapose and make use of their different sets of linguistic resources flexibly and creatively, informed by the need to engage pupils in teaching and learning processes. At the same time, they show how complementary schools seek to keep languages separate by insisting on the use of the community language only and privileging its standard version over regional, classed, youth and diasporic varieties. The authors argue that these two positions co-exist in the ideology and practice of complementary schools, thus underpinning different sets of values, attitudes and beliefs in relation to language, culture and heritage.

In Chapter Two, *Investigating the intersection of multilingualism and multimodality in Turkish and Gujarati literacy classes*, Vally Lytra, Peter Martin, Taşkın Baraç and Arvind Bhatt use field notes and still photography from classroom interaction to explore the ways pupils' and teachers' languages and language varieties form part of a wider landscape of communication in complementary school classrooms which integrates words with a range of modes available (eg image, writing, action, artefacts). Building on the work of Kress (1997, 2000), Kress and van Leeuwen (1996), Kress *et al* (2005) on multi-modal social semiotics, they illustrate how the participants' sets of linguistic and other semiotic resources are intertwined in their talk around texts in Turkish and Gujarati literacy classes. The authors conclude that the investigation of the intersection of multilingualism and multimodality can provide a useful point of entry into the reproduction of key aspects of the local inter-actional order of complementary school classrooms and foreground the tensions and contradictions around power, agency and the unequal distri-bution of linguistic and other resources between pupils and teachers.

In Chapter Three, *Literacy and socialisational teaching in Chinese comple-mentary schools*, Li Wei and Chao-Jung Wu discuss what they call 'socialisa-tional teaching' of literacy, which they see as impressing socio-cultural tradi-tions and values on pupils through mundane pedagogical literacy activities. Drawing on classroom exchanges, field notes and interviews with pupils and teachers, the authors demonstrate how a focus on such literacy activities can bring to the fore competing notions of language, culture and heritage be-tween the teacher and the parent generation on the one hand and the British-Chinese children and youth on the other.

In Chapter Four, *Abetare and dancing: the story of a partnership*, Raymonde Sneddon tells the story of a partnership between a mainstream school and an Albanian community organisation which has set up Albanian language and culture classes across several London boroughs. Sneddon uses extended field notes from the Albanian classes and interviews with the young people to des-cribe how pupils and teachers use different sets of linguistic resources in literacy learning and traditional folk dancing. She illustrates how the teacher's pedagogic practices, traditional teaching style and the use of imported teach-ing materials from Albania construct the literacy class as an almost exclu-sively Albanian space, while the dancing classes, although mainly in English, allow for the mixing and juxtaposition of languages. She shows that Albanian language and culture classes offer spaces for exploring language and culture, supporting the young people's bilingualism and developing their cultural, learner and multilingual identities.

In Chapter Five, *Grandmothers as orchestrators of early language and literacy lessons*, Mahera Ruby, Eve Gregory, Charmian Kenner and Salman Al-Azami transport us to the home of a Bangladeshi British family where the grand-mother has taken on the role of teacher as well as grandmother of the children in the immediate family and the wider neighbourhood. This chapter illustrates how teaching and learning takes place when the teacher is able to bridge home and complementary school settings by bringing them together in one site. They liken the grandmother to the conductor of an orchestra and each child to a musician who has a particular role to play. They describe what they call 'orchestrated learning', exploring how the grandmother/teacher teaches literacy in Bengali geared to each child's age and competence, while imparting cultural knowledge and religious practices.

### Processes of identity formation

Similar to mainstream schools, complementary schools are 'sites where ethnicity, culture, language use and the representation of identity are played out' (Miller, 2003:2). While (mainstream) schools have silenced 'the voices of subordinate groups whose primary language is not English and whose cultural capital is either marginalised or disparaged by the dominant culture of schooling' (Giroux, 1992:203), complementary schools open up spaces for children, parents and teachers to accept and reproduce but also contest and transform aspects of their identities associated with their heritage, cultural, religious, gender, age, institutional, learner and other affiliations (eg Creese *et al*, 2006; Creese *et al*, 2008; Francis *et al*, 2008). Creese *et al* (2006) argue for the case of Gujarati schools but this can be applied to other complementary schools as well:

> [they] provide an institutional context for young people to meet and consider (reproduce and contest) existing categories around nationality, culture, ethnicity, bilingualism and learning. They potentially provide their students with distinct institutional experiences different from mainstream schools. This is because complementary schooling provides a context for identity negotiation in bilingual contexts in which languages and linguistic repertoires are foregrounded in school mission statements (p40).

A central premise of this research on identity construction processes is shared by the contributors to this volume: language is a key representational resource for identity negotiation: it is through language (as well as other semiotic resources, as Lytra *et al* illustrate) that young people, their parents, teachers and other staff represent themselves and are represented by others. While drawing on a range of theoretical frameworks for conceptualising identity processes, the contributors converge on an understanding of identity as a dynamic on-going process that is always situated. Identity is not located in the individual and it is not a taken-for-granted bounded phenomenon; rather identities can co-exist, evolve and change but they can also be fragmented, imposed or found to be non-negotiable (Pavlenko and Blackledge, 2004).

In Chapter Six, *Constructing cultural and academic identities in community schools: a socio-cultural and dialogical approach*, Evangelia Prokopiou and Tony Cline draw on recent dynamic psychological approaches to identity and use cultural developmental theory (Valsiner, 2000) and the dialogical self theory (Hermans, 2001a) to explore the development of cultural and academic identities of Greek and Greek-Cypriot and Pakistani ethnic minority youth. Through interview data, they show how schools endorse a successful academic identity for pupils and seek to make links across educational contexts. They illustrate, however, that the pupils' cultural identity negotiations are shaped by different concerns and experiences: for those of Pakistani background, these are racism and religious discrimination whereas for the Greek and Greek-Cypriots these are fears of potential loss of one's community identity, language and culture.

Chapter Seven, *Chinese complementary school pupils' social and educational subjectivities*, by Becky Francis, Louise Archer and Ada Mau, adopts a broad poststructuralist approach (Chun, 1996; Foucault, 1972, 1980) to focus on how Chinese (Cantonese-speaking) young people's social and educational identities are discursively produced. They use interview data, to show how young people reproduce a notion of ethnic identity as constituted by language, reflecting perhaps the demographics of those attending complementary schools (eg second generation with at least one parent born overseas). They demonstrate the role of schools in supporting the children's diasporic cultural identities, providing them with the opportunity to engage in contemporary forms of youth cultural expression and developing their learner and learning identities.

In Chapter Eight, *Language choices: portraits of children's identity negotiations in a Brazilian Portuguese community school*, Ana Souza tells the story of three mixed heritage children through interview and interactional classroom data featuring teacher-pupil exchanges and informal talk among peers. Taking a social constructivist view of identity (Rao, 1999), she discusses the ways the three children draw on their different sets of linguistic resources to negotiate aspects of their learner identities. She concludes by stressing the important role the Brazilian Portuguese community school plays in providing mixed heritage children with a social, cultural and educational space where they can develop aspects of their social identities through learning the community language and simply by being with other Portuguese-speaking children.

### Policy and practice

Conteh *et al* (2007b) document the policy background for the management of bilingualism/multilingualism in Britain which has influenced the use, teaching and learning of community languages in mainstream and complementary schools over decades. *Education for All* (the Swann Report, DES, 1985), they maintain, transferred the responsibility of teaching community languages from primary and secondary schools to the communities heralding, as the authors argue, 'a long process of monolingualising within the curriculum as a whole' (p5). A series of policy documents thereafter further marginalised community languages and their teaching and learning in mainstream schools, and contributed to the deficit view of bilingualism/multilingualism (p5-7). Government policy has recently moved towards acknowledging the positive contribution complementary schools make to the educational experiences and worldviews of young people. Policy initiatives such as *Excellence and Enjoyment: a strategy for primary schools* (DfES, 2003a), *Every Child Matters* (DfES, 2003b) and *Aiming Higher* (DfES, 2003) provide hopeful signs for collaboration between complementary and mainstream schools and the development of bilingual pedagogies (p7-9; see also the on-going ESCR seminar series on *Complementary schools: towards evidence-based policies and practices*, 2008-2010; for further discussion of policy, Barradas, Conteh, Robertson in this volume).

In the Afterword to the special issue *Interaction in Complementary School Contexts*, Li Wei (2006) identifies at least two important areas of practice – also addressed in his book – where more research is needed. One area is related to pedagogy and classroom management and the other to teacher education and development (Conteh, Pantazi, Robertson this volume). As several chapters in this book illustrate (eg Blackledge and Creese, Li Wei and Wu, Sneddon, Souza), complementary schools draw on pedagogic practices and teaching styles that differ from those in the mainstream. While teachers, parents and school staff in complementary schools acknowledge these differences, there has been little support in the teachers' professional development and curriculum innovation (but see, for instance, the partnership projects for promoting community languages in complementary and mainstream schools in *Our Languages* project, 2007-2009 and the resources on community languages for teacher educators and student teachers available via the *Multiverse* website).

The chapters in this book may address different aspects of policy and practice but all concur with the need to develop closer links between complementary and mainstream schools, share good practice in teaching and learning and support professional development and curriculum innovation in complementary schools.

In Chapter Nine, *Teachers' developing theories and practices in Greek community schools*, Efstathia Pantazi traces the reflective cycle that a group of complementary school teachers went through as they identified the needs and responded to the linguistic and cultural diversity they encountered among their Greek and Greek-Cypriot heritage pupils. Using in-depth interview data collected by teachers on a five-year appointment to Greek community schools in London, Pantazi shows how teachers explore, reflect upon and develop their teaching theories and practices and modify their approaches to language teaching, culture and identity accordingly. She stresses the need for pre- and in-service mainstream teachers to experience the teaching and learning that goes on in complementary schools (and visa versa) so they can better understand the educational, social, cultural and identity needs of ethnic minority young people across learning contexts.

Chapter Ten, *Developing links between communities, schools and teacher training*, by Leena Helavaara Robertson, discusses a *Multiverse* funded project that sought to bring together a group of teacher trainee students with teachers from two community language schools and their local primary schools. Drawing on interviews, she illustrates how the teacher trainee students' visits shifted their perceptions of ethnic minority pupils and their learning and achievement and increased awareness of the role of complementary schools in developing community cohesion. Like Pantazi, she calls for collaborative projects that bring together different stakeholders in initial teacher education programmes to challenge long held assumptions that nourish a deficit view of bilingualism/multilingualism and also to challenge societal and institutional stereotypes about ethnic minority children and their educational trajectories.

In Chapter Eleven, *Linking community and mainstream schools: opportunities and challenges for Portuguese language and culture classes*, Olga Barradas examines the ways recent policy initiatives open up possible opportunities while also presenting challenges for the teaching and learning of community languages in general and Portuguese in particular. Using policy documents and interviews from young people attending Portuguese classes and their parents, she demonstrates how establishing closer links between complementary and mainstream schools not only enhances the children's learning and academic attainment across educational contexts but also improves community relations as a whole. She identifies three important challenges for Portuguese language and culture classes which can be extended to complementary schools more generally: the invisibility of complementary school teachers in mainstream schools, securing external funding, and its implications for determining who decides the content and teaching methodologies in complementary schools.

Chapter Twelve, *Making links across complementary and mainstream classrooms for primary children and their teachers* by Jean Conteh, is the concluding chapter, bringing together many of the themes addressed in the book. She weaves together observations and interviews with children attending a bilingual complementary school in Bradford and their parents, and with a group of bilingual mainstream teachers – some of whom also teach in complementary schools – to describe different ways they make links across learning contexts. She goes on to discuss recent policy initiatives about language and learning and the implications for developing bilingual pedagogies across complementary and mainstream classrooms which ultimately enhance the children's self-esteem and possibilities to succeed and considers the bilingual teachers' professional identities. Conteh concludes by arguing for the need to reconceptualise the links between children's learning in complementary and mainstream schools by foregrounding the actors (learners and teachers) and their developing identities, rather than the codes taught and learned.

This volume as a whole attests to the multiple roles complementary schools play in the lives of children, their families and communities, that go well beyond the maintenance of the community language and culture. Rather than reinforcing ethnic enclaves as they have often been accused of doing, it is clear that complementary schools provide vital spaces for the development and transformation of young people's multilingual resources, educational trajectories and identity options.

# Part I:
# Language and literacy practices

# 1

## Opening up flexible spaces: ideology and practice in complementary schools

*Adrian Blackledge and Angela Creese*

### Introduction

Hornberger (2005:606) suggests that it is essential for language educators to 'fill up implementational spaces with multilingual educational practices' in the face of restrictive policies, and views the rise of what she calls 'the heritage language initiative' as a movement which helps to 'solidify, support, and promote longstanding grassroots minority language maintenance and revitalisation efforts' (Hornberger, 2007:188). In their account of 'heritage language learners' in the United States, Hornberger and Wang (2008:6) adopt an ecological view of heritage language learners' identity. Specifically, they view heritage language learners as 'individuals with familial or ancestral ties to a language other than English who exert their agency in determining if they are heritage language learners of that language'. Hornberger (2007:189) argues that the heritage language initiative

> takes an ecological, resource view of indigenous, immigrant, ethnic, and foreign languages as living and evolving in relation to each other and to their environment and as requiring support lest any of them become further endangered.

May (2008:23) suggests that heritage language programmes 'can be regarded as an additive and strong bilingual approach', and notes that, increasingly, the majority of students in such programmes tend to be second language speakers of the target language, the result of previous patterns of language shift and loss of the heritage language. Garcia (2005:604) argues that complementary schools can offer an informal means to prise open a 'crack' in the educational homogenisation which is characteristic of national policy, allowing bilingual instruction to continue in the face of monolingualising ideologies. However, she also argues that complementary schools are 'a far cry from what we should be doing with the nation's bilingualism and biliteracy potential' (2005:604).

Kagan and Dillon (2008:151) note that there is as yet no standard approach to teaching heritage languages, and that the teaching of heritage language learners can be complicated by attitudes these students may encounter in the educational system. For example, heritage language teachers may insist on pure or standard forms, and in doing so stigmatise varieties spoken in the students' families.

Valdés *et al*, (2008) propose that a key challenge facing the field of heritage language teaching is that of determining the role that educational settings should play in language maintenance. Arguing that hegemonic beliefs about monolingualism and multilingualism are frequently embedded within educational institutions, they examine whether heritage language teaching may transmit 'nation-imagining beliefs and values that can often result in the alienation and marginalisation of the heritage students' (2008:107). These researchers investigated language ideologies in a Spanish language department in a university in the United States, and found that ideologies of language indirectly reproduced the ideological hegemony of the state. Everyday interaction in the department transmitted the message that (Spanish) monolingual-like behaviour was the ideal, and US Latinos must be reconstituted as imitation monolingual speakers of Spanish if they were to be valued.

Valdés *et al* (2008:125) concluded that 'the department echoes the existing nation-imagining beliefs of US society within which bilingualism – especially when developed in homes and communities by immigrant populations – is profoundly suspect'. While teaching literature in Spanish the department transmitted 'views that support the idealisation of the monolingual native, a view that, while focused on Spanish, nevertheless is complicit with the deep values and linguistic beliefs of American monolingualism' (*ibid*). Valdés *et al* propose that one of the reasons why such ideologies are commonly reproduced in such settings is that the teachers are often individuals raised in places where the language they teach is the dominant and/or national language. Besides their deep personal commitment to the languages they teach, they may have little knowledge or understanding of societal bilingualism, and 'give much attention to 'protecting' the language from contamination ... and to providing a model of a standard target language free of vulgar colloquial-isms and popular jargon' (p126).

Valdés *et al* suggest that heritage language teachers who are committed to the maintenance and teaching of their language may become intolerant of the contact varieties of the language used by heritage speakers because they have little understanding of language contact and bilingualism. They argue that teachers' fear of contamination and erosion in their own language may contribute to the scorn that they direct at bilinguals who, unlike the teachers, may be second or third generation speakers of the heritage language. Valdés *et al* suggest that language practices may be coloured by a national aesthetic that is concerned with the characteristic features of the original national lan-guage and culture. Ricento (2005) counsels that advocates for the promotion of heritage languages need to look critically at the assumptions in which they may be complicit, as heritage discourses may help promote the *status quo* with regard to the status and utility of languages other than English, viewing them as foreign.

In this chapter we engage with these as yet 'unexamined challenges' (Valdés *et al*, 2008:124) in heritage language teaching and learning in complementary schools, and suggest that complementary schools may open up spaces in which young people and their teachers use flexible multilingual practice, while simultaneously insisting on associations with standard versions of heri-tage languages. We see these positions co-existing in the ideology and prac-tice of complementary schools.

## Context

The research project we describe here is the same one as that discussed in the following two chapters. Four interlocking case studies focused on Gujarati schools in Leicester, Turkish schools in London, Cantonese and Mandarin schools in Manchester, and Bengali schools in Birmingham. The present chapter focuses on data collected in and around the Bengali schools in Birmingham.

Bengali complementary schools in Birmingham are managed and run by local community groups on a voluntary basis, usually in hired or borrowed spaces, with few resources. They cater for children between 4 and 16 years of age, and operate mainly in the evenings and at weekends. One of the specific aims of the research project was to investigate how the linguistic practices of students and teachers in complementary schools are used to negotiate young people's multilingual and multicultural identities.

5

In this chapter we consider two understandings of complementary schools which may at first sight appear to be contradictory, but which enjoy a relatively harmonious co-existence. First, complementary schools may be viewed as 'safe spaces' (Creese and Martin, 2006; Creese *et al*, 2006) where teachers and students engage in fluid linguistic practices which allow them to draw on a wide range of available resources in creating meaning. This 'trans-languaging' (Williams, 1996; Garcia, 2007, 2009) practice is associated with multicultural, transnational subject positioning. Characteristic of such an ideology is linguistic practice described as 'flexible bilingualism' (Blackledge and Creese, 2009; Creese and Blackledge, in press), 'dynamic bilingualism' (Garcia, 2009:54) or 'heteroglossia' (Bailey, 2007). Flexible bilingualism captures the heteroglossic nature of communication in the bilingual context of complementary schools. It leads us away from a focus on languages as distinct codes to a focus on the agency of individuals in a school community engaging in using, creating and interpreting signs to communicate to multilingual audiences. Second, we may view the schools as spaces which provide opportunities for students to learn not only a language but also the heritage associated with that language, its cultural practices, loyalties and affiliations. This heritage ideology focuses on the construction and maintenance of ethnic, cultural, linguistic, and national belonging. Characteristic of this ideology is an imperative to keep languages separate and pure as far as possible.

## Multilingual homes as translanguaging spaces

In this section we present examples of flexible language practice in non-institutional settings, particularly in the interactions of young people as they prepare to leave for complementary schools while still at home. These interactions demonstrate the usual practice of heteroglossic language use in students who attend complementary schools.

In Example 1 Aleha (10 years) and her sister Rumana are about to leave their house and say goodbye to their parents respectfully with the Arabic-derived 'salam alaikum'. Mainly English is used by Aleha with her older sister and her mother, while Sylheti is used with her father:

## Example 1

Aleha:     Rumana, come on. I'm going amma, salam alaikum
           <mother, salam alaikum>

           salam alaikum abba, zaairam aami
           <salam alaikum father. I'm going>

While 'I'm going' is spoken in English to her mother, Aleha uses Sylheti (the spoken language of North-East Bangladesh, and of the families participating in this research) to say the same thing to her father. Notable here is the unmarked and quite usual multilingualism of the interaction: English, Sylheti, and an Arabic-derived phrase enjoy a flexible and non-conflictual co-existence. We recorded many instances of flexible linguistic practice in the homes of students who attended the Bengali schools. In the following example Tamim, a 10-year-old boy, is asking his mother whether he is allowed to go on the school camping trip:

## Example 2

amma aami camping-e zaaitaam. aafne last year here disoin aamaare disoinnaa. aami camping zaaitaam aafne aamaare disenna

<mother, I want to go camping you allowed him last year but not me. I want to go camping you didn't allow me last year>

This is an unremarkable, common example of flexible language practice in the students' family settings, of the sort we heard on each occasion we audio-recorded the children and young people at home. Such multilingual practice at least partly constitutes the context for our investigation of multilingualism in the institutional setting of the complementary school.

We also recorded some of the students who attended the Bengali schools reading the Qur'an with their Qur'anic Arabic tutor. The tutor would visit the students' home to instruct them. In the following example the tutor has come to the home of Tamim (10 years), and Shazia (9 years), and the children are reciting Arabic terms along with him:

## Example 3

| | |
|---|---|
| Tutor: | qaribun, qareebun, qareeb [reads along with Shazia, often repeating the same words] re- yaa ze- yaa qaa ri- bun |
| Shazia: | six times forsi <I read it six times> |
| Tutor: | qaf zabar qaa, re zer ri, be pesh bu, nun, qareebun [spells the Arabic words. This is repeated many times] laam zabar laa |
| Tamim: | aami khaali ekhtaa mistake khorsi, ekhtaa mistake khorsi sir <I made only one mistake, only one mistake sir> |

Here the tutor is teaching the children the words in Arabic by repetition. Tamim uses Qur'anic Arabic, Sylheti and English together. None of the Arabic words are given a definition or meaning by the tutor. However, Tamim told us that although he was not able to understand as he was reading, the tutor would explain passages, and 'after I finish it, I am going to get an English version of the Qur'an so that I can understand every word of it'. Tamim read the verse fluently with little help from his tutor, and demonstrated (in Sylheti and English) his positive attitude to reading Arabic.

Characteristic of the interactions of the students we audio-recorded in and out of complementary school classrooms was a linguistic playfulness and creativity. Students engaged with and accessed a broad range of linguistic resources. Bangladeshi-heritage children watched Hindi films, and were familiar with Hindi songs. They sang along with the songs, and were able to express their preferences and dislikes. In the following example the two sisters Rumana and Aleha are watching a film just before going to Bengali class:

**Example 4**

[Rumana sings with the music on TV]

Rumana:   it's a funny movie that. this one, Hera Pheri. really funny, I like this song

Aleha:   I like [to baby sister] talk, talk, say amaar naam Durdana say amaar naam Durdana <say my name is Durdana>

Durdana:   one khe <who's there?>

Rumana:   [singing along in Hindi] wokkepaari, wokkepaari wokkepaari, wokkepaari, tumhare bina <without you> chaenna aaye <there's no peace> waakkepari

Here singing along with the Hindi film music seems to be a usual feature of the children's linguistic world, as they move in and out of English, Sylheti, and Hindi while listening to, participating in, and enjoying the Hindi film. At the same time they engage bilingually with their baby sister Durdana's attempts to speak into the digital recording device.

In this section we have seen that the students' usual linguistic practice is heteroglossic: that is, their usual talk, while largely in English, draws on a diverse range of resources. In the next section we consider institutional discourses about linguistic practice in the complementary schools.

**Language as heritage**

Teachers in the schools often expressed to us their fear that their students would lose their heritage language and culture unless languages were kept separate. This fear is based on evidence which demonstrates the gradual loss of community languages in immigrant communities over generations. Jaffe (2007:53) argues that when a minority community sees the 'tip in the direction of the dominant language' they do not choose to adopt current discourse patterns for their linguistic standard. Rather, 'authentic identity is anchored in the pre-shift society that existed before the economic, ideological and educational pressure that led to language shift' (*ibid*). Heller (2006:32) suggests that in seeking to break apart the monolithic identity of the state within which they search for a legitimate place, minority groups may construct a 'fictive unity', which effectively produces internally structures of hegemony similar to those against which they struggle. This helps explain why complementary schools might endorse the national culture of the pre-shift society, preferring an idealised version of the heritage culture to the diversity emerging in diasporic urban life (see also Chapters 3, 7). We frequently listened to the voices of those who considered their language to be part of their cultural heritage, and fundamental to their sense of themselves. We heard this argument again and again in interviews with the teachers and parents of the students:

## Example 5

Bengali is our mother land, where we come from, mainly we come from Bangladesh. Even if you are born in this country, it doesn't matter we need to know our mother language first. (parent interview)

For many of the parents and teachers, learning the language of the motherland held a symbolic significance beyond the utility of the language in the UK context. One of the teachers told us that there was a clear association between learning Bengali and affiliating to the heritage of Bangladesh:

## Example 6

From the national concern you should know Bengali, national Bengali the basic thing I'm not saying that he or she should be highly qualified in Bengali, national Bengali just the national thing, the basic thing. They should know like the alphabets, how to read. Sometimes if somebody speaks with them the national language they should be able to know what they've been saying. (teacher interview)

We frequently saw individual participants positioning themselves in relation to the 'ethnic, linguistic, and cultural loyalties' (Pavlenko, 2007:177) which they chose to emphasise. One of the senior teachers in the same school argued that learning Bengali was associated with maintaining knowledge of Bangladeshi 'roots':

## Example 7

We may have become British Bangladeshi or British Indians but we don't have fair skin and we cannot mix with them. We have our own roots and to know about our roots we must know our language. (teacher interview)

For both of these Bangladeshi-born teachers, teaching and learning Bengali was an important means of reproducing their heritage in the next generation. We heard an explicit rationale from administrators, teachers, and parents that a key aim of the schools was for the children to learn Bengali because knowledge of the national language carried features of Bangladeshi/Bengali heritage.

## Opening up ideological space for the standard language

When we interviewed the administrators and teachers in the schools they spoke emphatically about the need for children to learn Bengali, the standard, literate language of Bangladesh. This was frequently held to be oppositional to Sylheti, which was the spoken variety used by the families of students attending the Bengali schools. One of the school administrators was emphatic that Bengali was not the same as Sylheti, and that Sylheti should not be allowed to 'contaminate' the standard form. He was concerned that Sylheti forms were beginning to appear in the spelling and grammar of Bengali newspapers in UK, introducing 'thousands of spelling mistakes – Bengali newspapers I have seen in many places the spelling was wrong, sentence construction was wrong'. For the administrator non-standard resources were 'contaminating the language'. He made the following point about the necessity for children to learn standard Bengali:

## Example 8

I am always in favour of preserving languages and all these things. But it doesn't mean that this should contaminate other languages and give this more priority than the proper one. We have to preserve the proper one first, but we shouldn't make any compromise between these two. (administrator interview)

This was a frequent and strongly articulated argument that we heard in the complementary schools. The administrator of the other Birmingham school stated that:

## Example 9

Bhasha to bolle Bangla bhasha bolte hobe Sylheti kono bhasha naa <when you talk about language it means Bengali, Sylheti is not a language> (administrator interview)

For these respondents Bengali constituted a more highly valued set of linguistic resources than Sylheti, and was regarded as the proper language. Those who spoke Sylheti were often criticised by more educated people who spoke Bengali. Sylheti speakers were characterised by the administrator of one of the schools as members of the 'scheduled', or untouchable caste, people without rights or resources in the Indian sub-continent:

## Example 10

Publicraa ki dibe amar aapne especially bujhben amader desher je shob lok aashche ora kon category lok aashchilo, mostly from scheduled caste, gorib, dukhi krishokra aashchilo. oder maa baba o lekha pora interested naa oder chele meye raa o pora lekha interested naa. oraa baidhitamolok schoole jete hoe primary schoole sholo bochor porjonto jete hoe, ei jonne schoole jaai. <What will the public contribute? You [to the researcher] especially will understand what type of people came from our country. They belonged to the category of scheduled caste, they are the poor, the deprived, farmers. Their parents were not interested in education nor are the children interested. They go to school because it's compulsory>. (administrator interview)

Regarded as the least educated group in society, with no resources of any kind, Sylheti speakers are considered to be the lowest of the low (Borooah *et al*, 2007; Borooah, 2005; Kijima, 2006). Here linguistic features were viewed as reflecting and expressing broader social images of people. More than one of the teachers argued that children should learn Bengali for 'moral reasons'. Irvine and Gal (2000:37) suggest that 'participants' ideologies about language locate linguistic phenomena as part of, and evidence for, what they believe to be systematic behavioural, aesthetic, affective, and moral contrasts among the social groups indexed'. Irvine and Gal propose that a semiotic process of iconisation occurs, in which linguistic features that index social groups appear to be iconic representations of them, as if a linguistic feature depicted or displayed a social group's inherent nature or essence. Pujolar (2007:78), referring to a different socio-historical context, makes the point that language policy may operate to foster knowledge of some languages, 'but delegitimise or ignore other languages and other forms of multilingual competence and performance'. Patrick (2007:127) similarly finds that in arguing in support of a particular language, 'speakers can be locked into fixed or essentialised notions of identity, 'authenticity' and place, which provide no recognition of mobile, postcolonial speakers'.

It was clear that for some of our respondents not all linguistic resources were equally valued, and while some sets of linguistic resources were considered to be a language, others were not. Bourdieu and Darbel (1991:112) argue that some more powerful groups provide 'an essentialist representation of the division of their society into barbarians and civilised people'. Here the fact of speaking Sylheti, rather than Bengali, appeared to index the Sylheti group in particularly negative terms, despite the relative similarities between the Bengali and Sylheti sets of linguistic resources. Whilst some speakers in our study considered Sylheti to be quite different from Bengali, others regarded the two sets of resources as indistinguishable.

As we have seen, there were several instances of participants commenting on the differences between Sylheti and Bengali in terms of social status and value, but not everyone agreed about the extent to which these sets of linguistic resources were distinct. While the administrator of one of the schools argued that Bengali and Sylheti were 'completely different', a student's mother said they were 'thoraa different' <a little different>, while other parents also held this view, saying they were 'little bit different thaake' <only> and even 'the same'. Here there was clear disagreement about the nature and extent of the differences between the sets of linguistic resources used by the students' parents at home, and the literate version of the language taught in the complementary school classrooms. That is, there was disagreement about the permeability of the boundaries between languages.

These differences of perception were likely to be ideological. Those who argued that the languages were completely different from each other were speakers of the prestige language, unwilling to allow the lower status language to contaminate their linguistic resources. Those who argued that the languages were almost the same as each other were speakers of Sylheti, which was held to index the lower status, less educated group.

On many occasions children demonstrated their awareness of ideological differences between Sylheti and Bengali. The following example is from field notes taken during the first week of observation. The teacher is working with a group of 10 and 11-year-old children:

## Example 11

There is a discussion about linguistic differences between Sylheti and Bengali, focusing on the phrase 'I have a friend'. Shazia says to the teacher: we say 'aamaar shoi aasoin' (Sylheti), but you say 'aamaar ekti shoi aase' (Bengali). She also gives an example in English, Sylheti and Bengali: 'aamaar ekti friend aase'. The Bengali phrase is accompanied by much eye-rolling and eyebrow-raising from Shazia, and intonation which indicates that speaking the phrase in Bengali is associated with a different social class. That is, Bengali appears to be associated with putting on airs, showing off, or sophistication. This is meta-linguistic discussion at a thoughtful and playful level for 10-year-olds.

When she says 'we don't use this language', Shazia appears to distinguish the children and their families from the teacher. Here the children, and Shazia in particular, show an understanding that Sylheti and Bengali are different from each other, and also that they index different social groups and values. However, even in this instance where linguistic differences are explicitly marked by children, and acknowledged by teachers, the simple dichotomy between Sylheti and Bengali breaks down: Shazia borrows the Bengali word 'shoi' in her example of Sylheti, and uses the more polite form of the Sylheti verb 'aasoin' in her example of Bengali. Despite the clear ideological differences between Sylheti and Bengali for many of our participants, the varieties were frequently mixed in their linguistic practices.

## Teaching heritage in flexible spaces

The rationale of the schools was put into practice in the classroom through a pedagogy which frequently introduced heritage content in the context of teaching Bengali. Here heritage content included narratives of national belonging, and the introduction of national symbols of Bangladesh. In Example 12 T is the teacher, and Shahnaz a 10-year-old girl:

## Example 12

| | |
|---|---|
| T: | Bangladesher teen taa national day aache, jaatio dibosh <Bangladesh has three national days, national events> national day not national anthem |
| Shahnaz: | independence day |
| T: | etaa Banglae ki bolbe shaadhinota dibosh Ekushey February shohid dibosh aage bolo Ekushey February shohid dibosh <in Bangla it is shaadhinota dibosh 21st February is shohid dibosh first say 21st February is shohid dibosh> |
| Shahnaz: | Ekushey February shohid dibosh |
| T: | er pore aashlo shaadhinota dibosh <after that comes shaadhinotaa dibosh> independence day, independence day is not Bangla, it is English. Banglae holo <in Bangla it is> shaadhinota dibosh |
| Shahnaz: | chaabbish-e March <26th March> |
| T: | shaadhinota dibosh |

Shahnaz:     chaabbish-e March <26th March>

T:          lastly nine months we fought against Pakistani collaborator

Shahnaz:     language day

T:          language day holo ekushey February. Chaabbish March
            independence day. Sholoi December, after nine months bijoy
            dibosh <victory day> Pakistani occupied army ke aamraa
            surrender korchi <we made the occupied forces of Pakistan
            surrender their arms> Al Badr against our independence war ke
            aamraa chutaaisi <we chased them out> How many national
            days in Bangladesh?

Shahnaz:     three

T:          Bangladesher jaatio dibosh koiti? <how many national days in
            Bangladesh?>

Shahnaz:     teen ti <three>

T:          Shaadhinota dibosh ebong bijoy dibosh chilo 1971. Bhasha
            dibosh chilo 1952. Aar bhaasha dibosh kon din chilo 52. Tokhon
            amraa choto <independence day and victory day was in 1971.
            Language day was in 1952. Language day was 52 when we were
            young> Inshaallah eta every day jodi aamraa every day discuss
            kori taahole bhaalo <by the grace of God it is good if we discuss
            this every day> (classroom video-recording)

Here the teacher instructs the students through content which refers to a
narrative of collective remembering in relation to the nation. Curriculum
content here is strongly nationalistic, and appears to have the aim of instilling
in the young language learners an understanding of key dates and events in
the making of the Bangladeshi nation. The 10-year-old student seems to have
some pre-existing knowledge of the historical context, and is prepared to
volunteer this. For example she offers the date of Bangladeshi independence
from West Pakistan, and is confidently able to do so in Bengali. The teacher
moves comfortably between Bengali and English within and between sentences, and in his final statement also uses the common Islamic expression
'Inshallah', derived from Arabic. The young student tends to respond in
English when the teacher asks a question in English, and in Bengali when the
teacher asks a question in Bengali. Language teaching here invents for the
students a sense of national belonging which is firmly rooted in narratives of
collective memory. The teacher's stories of poignant martyrdoms and heroic
victories serve to reproduce the national memory and imagination (Anderson,
1983). Here the process of teaching Bengali is intimately interwoven with the

process of teaching symbolic representations of Bangladesh, as knowledge of the national/cultural symbols, like knowledge of the Bengali language, comes to represent Bengali heritage.

In Example 13 another teacher is teaching language through cultural heritage content, reminding students of some iconic symbols of the nation:

## Example 13

| | |
|---|---|
| T: | Halima hoiseni? Mone aache goto shopta Bangladesher raajdhanir naamki<br><finished Halima? remember from last week the name of the capital of Bangladesh?> |
| S1: | Dhaka |
| T: | Bangladesher jaatio maach <Bangladeshi national fish?> |
| S1: | ilish |
| T: | Bangladesher jaatio phol <national fruit> big one, yellow colour |
| St: | pumpkin |
| T: | big one, yellow thaake taarpore khaaoaa jaae<br><big one, it's yellow and you can eat it> |
| S2: | kaathol |
| T: | kaathol ke ki bole, kaathaal<br><what is kaathol called, kaathaal><br><br>Bangladesher shob theke boro nodi<br><the largest river of Bangladesh> |
| S1: | Meghna |
| T: | Sylheter shob theke boro nodi, Surma<br><the largest river in Sylhet, Surma> |
| S1: | Surma |
| T: | Bangladesher shob theke boro nodi<br><the largest river of Bangladesh> |
| S1: | Surma |
| T: | Bangladesher shob theke boro nodi, Meghna<br><the largest river of Bangladesh is Meghna> |
| S1: | Meghna |
| | (audio-recording) |

Here the teacher moves easily and unhesitatingly between Bengali, Sylheti and English. He corrects the student's Sylheti version of the word for jack-fruit, offering the Bengali version in its place 'kaathol ke ki bole, kaathaal'. However, he is quite prepared to use Sylheti in the informal business of class-room organisation, eg 'Halima hoiseni?'. Similarly, he uses English alongside Bengali, apparently without any concern that the purity of the national language will be endangered, eg 'big one, yellow thaake taarpore khaaoaa jaae'.

## Conclusion

Our argument in this chapter has been that students who attend comple-mentary schools often draw on a wide range of linguistic resources in their daily lives, especially in domestic settings and peer interactions. This flexible language practice enables them to access diverse resources which they use together to create meanings. Secondly, we have demonstrated that the stated ideological positions of the complementary schools call for languages to be kept separate, because the Bengali language symbolises Bangladeshi cultural heritage and nationhood, and may be contaminated by contact with English and/or Sylheti. These findings resonate with those of Valdes *et al* (2008) who found that, while teachers of heritage languages may have deep personal commitment to the languages they teach, they may have little knowledge or understanding of societal bilingualism, and give much attention to protect-ing the language from contamination in order to pass it on to the next genera-tion in its existing form. However, this is certainly not the whole story to be told from our research. In contrast, we found that, while the schools certainly taught Bangladeshi nationalism and cultural heritage in direct, explicit terms, this was done through a flexible use of language in which both teachers and students drew on a wide range of linguistic resources which were used to-gether and interchangeably. That is, the stated ideology of the schools was not always consistent with the practices of those who inhabited them.

Our observations in the wider study of eight schools in Birmingham, Lei-cester, London, and Manchester raised questions about heritage, the re-membered nation, and the transmission of languages which carry the weight of culture and distant territories. Those who take responsibility for maintain-ing and transmitting their languages to the next generation invest in a multi-lingual future, but not necessarily a version of multilingualism which is acceptable to their students. We saw how languages often come to have different meanings for the young people who attend complementary school classes. Flexible verbal repertoires enabled the students to negotiate subject positions which may at times seem to be at odds with the discourses of the complementary schools.

However, as we have seen in the present chapter, there were many other occasions on which flexible multilingual practice was a feature of linguistic practice in the teaching of cultural heritage. In fact the linguistic practice of the teachers and students in the institutional setting was not very different from that of the students at home. Garcia (2009:8) argues for flexible bilingual classroom practice, as 'the language practices of bilinguals are interrelated and expand in different directions to include the different communicative contexts in which they exist'.

In this chapter we raise the possibility that complementary schools may both open up spaces in which young people and their teachers are able to engage in flexible multilingual practice, while at the same time insisting on reified ideological associations with standard versions of heritage languages. These positions are entirely compatible, as evidenced by their harmonious co-existence in complementary schools.

### *Note on transcription*
In keeping with the theoretical approach to linguistic practice which emerged from this work, we make no distinction between different languages in the transcribed data. We represent speech in romanised transliteration.

| | |
|---|---|
| speech | transcribed speech |
| &lt;speech&gt; | translated speech |
| CAPITALS | loud |
| ( ) | speech inaudible |
| [ ] | stage directions |

# 2

# Investigating the intersection of multilingualism and multimodality in Turkish and Gujarati literacy classes

*Vally Lytra, Peter Martin, Taşkın Baraç and Arvind Bhatt*

## Introduction

This chapter draws on two ESRC funded projects which explored multilingualism in complementary schools (Martin *et al*, 2004; Creese *et al*, 2008). One of the research aims that straddled both projects was to investigate the range of linguistic practices across contexts in complementary schools. We extend this research aim to look at the intersection of multilingualism and multimodality in Turkish and Gujarati complementary school literacy classes. Although we acknowledge that exploring the participants' (teachers and pupils) multimodal practices was not part of the initial research aims of the projects, we have been inspired by an increasing acceptance within educational research that multilingual interaction is more than simply the juxtaposition of sets of linguistic resources. Our aim is to show how languages and language varieties form part of a wider landscape of communication in complementary school classrooms which integrates words with a range of modes available (eg image, writing, moving image, action, artefacts). As a number of recent studies have illustrated (Bezemer, 2008; Flewitt, 2005; Lytra, forthcoming; Kenner, 2004; Kress *et al*, 2005; Pahl, in press), the multimodal analysis of classroom interaction is key to making sense of the participants' linguistic resources and practices across different classroom settings.

Following Pahl and Rowsell's lead (2006), we take multimodality as 'communication in the widest sense, including gesture, oral performance, artistic, linguistic, digital, electronic, graphic and artifact-related' (p6). Rather than separating the participants' linguistic and other semiotic resources and highlighting the boundaries between them, we seek to show how they are combined during the lesson. Our theoretical antecedents can be traced back to the work of Kress (1997, 2000), Kress and van Leeuwen (1996) and Kress *et al* (2005), who sought to extend the remit of a social semiotics approach to include multimodality. Multimodal social semiotics, as it is widely named, focuses on signs of all kinds, in all forms, the sign-makers and the social environments in which these signs are produced (Kress *et al*, 2005:22). Multimodal social semiotics views linguistic signs (both monolingual and multilingual) as part of a wider repertoire of modal resources which sign-makers have at their disposal. In this approach, language is seen as a central mode of communication but at the same time it is examined in relation to other modes that sign-makers can choose from for meaning making and social affiliation (see Lytra forthcoming for further discussion).

In this chapter, we explore the intersection of teachers and pupils' multilingual and multimodal practices in order to trace the ways they draw on the complex and multi-layered combination of communicative channels, including talk. The focus on the intersection of multilingualism and multimodality enables us to begin to capture the complex web of the participants' semiotic resources and explore how they are meshed together and work to create 'an ensemble of semiotic resources' (Pahl, 2008:17). Moreover, it allows us to probe into the textual and material dimensions for meaning making as well as the different ways that semiotic resources, practices and discourses become adapted to local contexts and also how locally inflected meanings are tied to global contexts (Pahl and Rowsell, 2006). Our focus is less on text production and more on the talk around texts and how the participants' combination of semiotic resources is mediated by texts in classroom interaction. Following Street (1993), we take a view of literacy as social practice situated culturally and historically in time and space rather than as a neutral set of skills to be acquired.

In the following sections, we briefly outline our methodology and present the Turkish and Gujarati communities and complementary schools in London and Leicester respectively. Drawing on field notes and still photography, we set out to explore the different ways teachers and pupils weave their multilingual and multimodal resources in literacy classes. We conclude by inquiring into the potential of this approach for classroom interaction in complementary school literacy classes.

## Methodological considerations

Our research takes an ethnographically informed case study approach that aims at foregrounding the perspectives of the participants. We draw on two studies, the first of which focused exclusively on Gujarati complementary schools in Leicester (Martin *et al*, 2004). Building on this, the second study expanded its scope to include four ethno-linguistic communities, two of which were Turkish (Cypriot-Turkish and mainland Turkish-speaking) in London and Gujarati in Leicester (Creese *et al*, 2008; also Blackledge and Creese and Li Wei and Wu in this volume).

In both studies, we collected data in a range of school settings. Besides participant observations, we digitally-recorded and video-recorded pupils in their classrooms, assemblies and break-times. We also digitally-recorded and video-recorded teachers working with pupils in their classrooms and video-recorded important school rituals and events. We interviewed the pupils, their parents, teachers and the schools' managing committees. Throughout the duration of the field-work we collected documentary data relating to each school's policy, planning and curriculum and still photography. Informed consent was solicited prior to and throughout the data collection. We draw on field notes written up in the form of analytic vignettes (Erickson, 2000) and still photography.

## Turkish and Gujarati complementary schools

Turkish- and Gujarati-speaking communities in Britain share similarities but also significant differences. Both are highly diverse and heterogeneous communities whose members have different religious affiliations, linguistic backgrounds, migration trajectories and educational and socio-economic capital and colonial ties with Britain. More specifically, Turkish-speaking communities are comprised of at least four groups with distinct migration histories and linguistic resources: Cypriot Turks, Turks from mainland Turkey, Turkish-speaking Kurds from Turkey and Turkish-speaking people who have moved to Britain from other EU countries. It is estimated that about 180,000-200,000 Turkish-speaking people are currently living in Britain, the majority concentrated in and around London (Mehmet Ali, 2001). The Gujarati-speaking population in Britain includes Hindu, Muslim, Jain and Christian communities. In the east midlands city of Leicester, Gujarati East Africans comprise the largest segment of this, and amount to about one fifth of Leicester's total population. Singh (2003) reports that over 20,000 East African and Ugandan Asians, who were expelled from Kenya and Uganda as a result of the Africanisation policies, arrived in the city between 1968 and 1973 (p45). In addition to the Gujarati speakers from Africa, a smaller number of settlers arrived direct from India.

The Turkish and Gujarati-speaking communities in London and Leicester have sought to maintain their distinctive cultures and languages by setting up complementary schools. These schools are organised, funded and maintained by the communities with minimal or no help from the local or national governments. The two Turkish complementary schools were located in East and West London respectively. Both schools were founded in the late 1980s and have between 110 to 250 children. The three Gujarati complementary schools had a long standing tradition of providing support for cultural and linguistic maintenance in Leicester. Indeed, one of the schools was the focus of fieldwork in both aforementioned studies.

## Two vignettes of multilingual and multimodal classrooms

The use of the teachers and pupils' multilingual and multimodal resources in classroom interaction often emerged in what appeared to be a teacher controlled classroom interactional order that had some of the following features: teachers made use of the traditional pattern of classroom talk where the teacher initiates, pupils respond and the teacher then provides feedback (ie the IRF sequence). Moreover, they made use of substitution drills (eg vocabulary building and grammar exercises) and the reading of texts on various topics followed by a set of reading comprehension questions checking meaning. As a result, classroom discourse tended to encourage decontextualised knowledge and modelling and chorus-style responses to teacher prompts (Creese *et al*, 2008). While these features of classroom discourse were pervasive, we also acknowledge the plurality of discourses in complementary school classrooms (Blackledge and Creese forthcoming; Lytra and Baraç, 2008; Lytra and Martin, 2009). This plurality of discourses has been nicely captured by Bernstein's (2000) distinction between an official 'vertical discourse' and a local 'horizontal discourse'. As Luk (2008) explains, 'while 'vertical discourse' takes the form of a coherent, explicit and systematically principled structure, 'horizontal discourse' 'entails a set of strategies which are local, segmentally organised, context specific and dependent' (p157) and represents the users' everyday lived experiences' (p127). In this chapter, we focus on the official 'vertical discourses' to explore how participants combine their multilingual and multimodal resources in literacy classes.

Although our observations reveal that Turkish and Gujarati classrooms share many similarities in terms of the official 'vertical discourses' available to participants, they also have at least one important difference that has implications in the ways teaching and learning took place. The default mode of classroom interaction in Turkish classrooms was (standard) Turkish, while in Gujarati classrooms it was a mixture of Gujarati and English. Elsewhere (Lytra and Martin, 2009), we discuss in more detail some of the broader socio-historical and local contextual parameters for the divergent language use in Turkish and Gujarati classrooms. For the purposes of this chapter, suffice it to say that this difference could be traced back to differences in the socio-historical context (eg migration trajectories, colonial legacy), socio-economic and educational contexts (eg access to educational, linguistic and symbolic resources and educational/professional achievement) as well as the local complementary school context (eg teachers' linguistic and professional backgrounds, attitudes towards the use of English and the community language and its regional and diasporic varieties inside and outside school settings). At the same time, we acknowledge that participants could draw in varying degrees upon a much wider range of linguistic resources besides English, Gujarati and (standard) Turkish:

- languages (German, Qur'anic Arabic, Hindi, Swahili, Sanskrit, French and other instructed foreign languages taught in mainstream schools);
- regional, classed and diasporic varieties of Turkish and Gujarati (Cypriot-Turkish and other regional varieties of Turkish, *Londralı* <London> Turkish, Leicester Gujarati);
- regional and classed varieties of English (London, Leicester);
- youth varieties (South Asian English, talk appropriated from hip hop and other forms of popular culture, the mass media and digital technology, urban street cultures and participation in multilingual/multicultural peer groups).

Teachers and pupils in complementary school classrooms attached different sets of values to different sets of linguistic resources (cf Heller, 2007, see also Blackledge and Creese in this volume). These different sets of values were influenced by as well as reproduced existing linguistic hierarchies inside and outside complementary school classrooms. For instance, the community language in its standard form was considered superior to its regional and diasporic varieties. In classroom practice, linguistic hierarchies often led participants to compartmentalise their different sets of linguistic resources based on the pedagogic principle that languages are best taught separately. At the same time, participants crossed linguistic boundaries and engaged in multilingual practices where they juxtaposed and mixed different sets of linguistic resources as well as talked about their knowledge of languages and literacies (see also Blackledge and Creese in this volume).

In the following classroom vignettes, we illustrate how some of the participants' above-mentioned linguistic resources formed part of a web of semiotic resources which they used in literacy teaching. The first classroom vignette comes from a Turkish classroom. All the children are around 10 years old and have been born in the UK. They are of Cypriot-Turkish, mainland Turkish and mixed heritage. Their teacher, Ercan Bey is on a five year appointment by the Turkish Ministry of Education to Britain. He has been teaching this class for a whole year and seems to get along very well with all the children. The vignette begins as he introduces a writing task. Note that all names are pseudonyms throughout.

Turkish classroom vignette 1

Ercan Bey asks the children to write a short story in Turkish where they will practice the pronouns they have focused on earlier in the lesson. The teacher has made a grid with the pronouns on the white board and has asked the pupils to copy it into their notebooks (see figure 1 below).

| | | Yalın | -i hali | -e hali | -de hali | -den hali |
|---|---|---|---|---|---|---|
| I. Kişi | Tekil | Ben | Beni | Bana | Bende | Benden |
| | Çoğul | Biz | Bizi | Bize | Bizde | Bizden |
| II. Kişi | Tekil | Sen | Seni | Sana | Sende | Senden |
| | Çoğul | Siz | Sizi | Size | Sizde | Sizden |
| III. Kişi | Tekil | O | Onu | Ona | Onda | Ondan |
| | Çoğul | Onlar | Onları | Onlara | Onlarda | Onlardan |

**Figure 1: Whiteboard with Turkish personal pronouns**

First, the teacher models how he wants the children to write the short story by recounting a short story of his own using some of the personal pronouns. Then, it's the children's turn to produce their stories in the form of a written narrative. As the children are busy putting their stories together, they ask the teacher clarification questions: they tend to ask their questions in Turkish (sometimes with a Cypriot-Turkish inflection) or English. The teacher nearly always responds in (standard) Turkish although his speech bears traces of a regional accent from South East Turkey and routinely reminds them *Türkçe konuş* <speak Turkish> and stay on task. In their clarification questions, I notice that the teacher and the children constantly refer to the table with the personal pronouns on the whiteboard and to the teacher's model of the short story. When they finish writing their stories in their notebooks the teacher asks for volunteers to read them aloud. Ayten is very eager and volunteers to go first. I've noticed she always wants to speak, answer the teacher and her peers' questions and read aloud her course work in class. She reads in a loud clear voice with a Cypriot-Turkish inflection. After this activity is over the teacher tells them they will play a modified version of Chinese whispers.

(from field notes 06/05/06)

The second classroom vignette comes from a Gujarati classroom. The children are 8 to 10 years old and have been born in the UK. Their teacher, Rashmaben, spent many years teaching in Kenya prior to coming to the UK. She is also a mainstream primary school teacher. She has a great rapport with the children who all seem very keen to learn. The teacher is illustrating how to write Gujarati letters.

### Gujarati classroom vignette

Once the teacher has written the date on the whiteboard, she asked the students to copy it into their books. But she stops them to explain in English about writing in Gujarati, she says: 'When we write in Gujarati listen everybody these are the lines'. She then draws three parallel, horizontal lines on the whiteboard and continues: 'ok, when you want to write your name, don't write on top of the line hang your letters. When you write in English you write on top of it. In Gujarati, you hang on the line like when you hang your clothes you hang Gujarati letters on the line'. [Gujarati has a non-linear script derived from Devnagari script. Whereas Devnagari uses a line to hang the letters from, Gujarati has dispensed with the straight line but keeps the tradition of hanging the letters from the line written on the page, though this is not strictly necessary.]

The students all write the dates in their note books. I look at the boy sitting next to me and he has done it and I note he's followed the teacher by hanging his letters under the line. The teacher then writes the letter S in Gujarati on the whiteboard. [Here the teacher uses the English letter S as a basis for teaching Gujarati orthography which includes the shape of S to form some of the consonants.] She asks the students in English what sound this represents and not everyone appears to know. She writes next to S = 'da' (see figure 2 below). She then goes on to explain, 'now you write 'da' ... put a stroke through like this ... what does it become?' She puts a stroke through S and elicits that the new letter represents the sound 'ka'. She then asks what two 'das' [one on top of the other] represent and one student answers [the sound] 'ha'. The teacher then relates that these letters are called family members as they all come from one family. She asks the students why and one student responds 'because they all look alike'. The teacher then uses the metaphor of the walking stick to indicate how the addition of /l/ lengthens the sounds 'da' to 'daa' and 'ka' to 'kaa'.

(from field notes 17/05/2003)

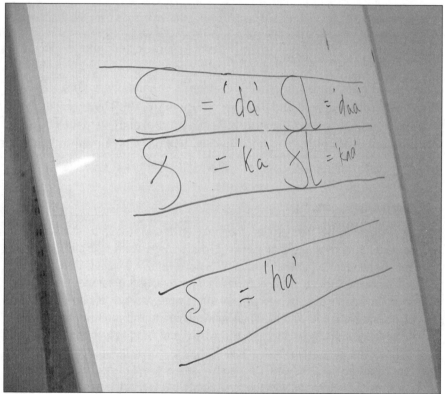

**Figure 2: Whiteboard with Gujarati letters and Roman transliteration**

The two classroom vignettes illustrate how teachers and pupils draw upon different semiotic resources and modes, including writing, speech, image, the body in performance and manipulate artefacts during literacy teaching and learning. In the Turkish classroom vignette, we observe how participants perform the writing task multilingually, making use of the standard form of the community language, its regional varieties as well as English. The children accomplish the writing task by making requests for clarification in (standard) Turkish but also occasionally in Cypriot-Turkish or English. The teacher, in turn, responds almost exclusively in (standard) Turkish, although his accent bears unmistakeable traces of his regional South East Turkish background. Although the young people may use both English and Turkish (and its regional varieties) to clarify and negotiate aspects of the writing task, the narrative they produce and read out is in (standard) Turkish only. The legitimacy of (standard) Turkish is further enhanced by the teacher's reminders to 'speak Turkish' throughout the writing task.

At the same time, our observations capture to some extent how the linguistic dimension of the literacy activity is closely intertwined with its textual dimension. The children and the teacher employ different linguistic resources in the process of writing the story which are combined with the manipulation of artefacts (eg the image of the personal pronouns on the whiteboard and the teacher's oral model of what such a short story should look like).

In the vignette illustrating the act of writing in the Gujarati classroom, we notice the centrality of English in classroom interaction as well as the regular alternation between codes and modes. As Kenner (2004) argues, 'handwriting has often been thought of as a purely mechanical skill. Yet, the act of writing is cultural, involving both body and mind' (p74). The vignette reveals how Rashmaben, the teacher, combines the verbal mode (English) to compare the act of writing in English and Gujarati and explain the intricacies of Gujarati script (ie hanging one's letters) and its cultural significance with gesture and the graphic mode as she juxtaposes Gujarati and transliterated Gujarati scripts on the whiteboard. The children respond to her questions in English and Gujarati as they copy the Gujarati and the transliterated Gujarati letters in their notebooks.

Our observations regarding the ways the participants' linguistic resources intertwine with their visual, graphic and kinaesthetic resources chime with Kress's claim that 'learning to produce and interpret written graphic symbols is a multimodal experience' (Kress, 1997, 2000 reported in Kenner, 2004:75). Throughout the vignette, we notice the teacher and the children using their multilingual and multimodal resources to produce and reproduce the type of strokes to be used as well as the shape, size and placement on the line of Gujarati letters.

Although the two vignettes describe different activities, they illustrate how participants combine sets of linguistic and multimodal resources to accomplish the lesson, including the body in performance. Here we draw upon and extend Bauman's concept of 'verbal performance' seen as linguistic practice that is 'situated, interactional, and communicatively motivated' (Bauman, 2000:1). Bauman (2000) goes on to define verbal performance as

> ... a special mode of situated communicative practice, resting on the assumption of accountability to an audience for a display of communicative skill and efficacy. In this sense of performance, the act of expression is put on display, objectified, marked out to a degree from its discursive surroundings and opened up to interpretive scrutiny and evaluation by the audience' (*ibid*).

A case in point is Ayten's reading of her short story after the completion of the writing task in the Turkish classroom vignette. Following Bauman (2000), Ayten's performance is marked out by its discursive surroundings though prosodic cues; she reads in a loud clear voice. While Bauman's understanding of performance privileges the linguistic aspect, we could argue based on previous classroom observations that Ayten's reading includes the body in performance (eg orienting her gaze towards her audience, standing up or coming to the front of the class). In this respect, her reading could be seen not simply as a verbal performance but as a multisemiotic one. Even more so, we propose to view the teacher's illustration of the Gujarati and transliterated Gujarati scripts in the Gujarati classroom vignette as a multisemiotic performance.

Her illustration of the Gujarati script resonates with Kenner's (2004) description of the teaching of handwriting in France. Kenner explains how the teaching of handwriting is based on a holistic philosophy called *le graphisme* which she translates as 'the act of writing' understood as '*un acte complexe* (a complex act) involving *une geste delicate* (a delicate movement)' (p74). Although our vignette does not capture as fully how the children drew upon their different semiotic resources, including the body in performance, to reproduce the Gujarati letters in their note books, we could extend our observations to them too.

## Concluding discussion

In this chapter, we have shown how, by paying close attention to the ways different languages and language varieties intersected with the participants' multimodal resources, we were able to provide a more nuanced and multi-layered understanding of Turkish and Gujarati literacy classes. The focus on the intersection of the participants' multilingual and multimodal resources allowed us to explore instances of the official 'vertical' classroom discourse where children and their teachers showcased aspects of their rich and complex semiotic repertoires. For instance, in the Turkish vignette, we illustrated how pupils juxtaposed (standard) Turkish, its regional variety (Cypriot-Turkish) and English to make clarification requests in Turkish literacy classes that were frequently dominated by (standard) Turkish. Moreover, we showed how the juxtaposition of different linguistic resources was combined with the manipulation of the image of the personal pronouns on the whiteboard and the teacher's oral model of the narrative genre.

In the Gujarati vignette, we demonstrated how the teacher and the pupils drew connections between the act of writing in Gujarati and English and how their linguistic resources were meshed with their visual, graphic and kinaesthetic resources in producing the Gujarati letters on the whiteboard and then reproducing them in their notebooks. Moreover, our focus on the intersection of the participants' linguistic and multimodal resources allowed us to re-conceptualise some of these instances of the official vertical classroom discourse as multisemiotic performances instead of solely verbal performances (eg Ayten's reading aloud of her story and Rashmaben's illustration of the Gujarati and transliterated Gujarati scripts on the whiteboard).

This focus also highlighted some of the tensions and contradictions about what counts as legitimate resources, codes and modes of communication in complementary school classrooms and how these tensions and contradictions are linked to broader social contexts (see also Blackledge and Creese; Li Wei and Wu in this volume). The following short Turkish classroom vignette brings them into sharp focus. This is a GCSE class. Most pupils are of Cypriot-Turkish heritage as is their teacher, Adem Bey. Prior to the vignette he has asked the pupils to read silently a text about Istanbul from their textbook and then do the first set of reading comprehension questions.

Turkish classroom vignette 2

The pupils are quietly working on the assigned task. As they are jotting down their answers in their note books, I see one girl asking Adem Bey for a pen. Instead of saying that she wants a pen she uses gestures, mimicking the act of writing. The teacher responds in the following way: 'Biz buna 'tükenmez' deriz. Aferin bakın Selma. Size her zaman söylediğımı uyguluyor. Türkçe konuşalım diyorum ya 'penna' dememek için bana işaret etti' <We call this [showing a pen] *tükenmez*. Well done Selma. You did what I always tell you to do. You know I tell you to speak Turkish all the time and Selma taking my advice used gestures to show me what she wanted instead of saying *penna*>. There is no reaction from the pupils and the teacher starts doing the reading comprehension questions with the whole of the class.

(from field notes 29/04/06)

We observe that the privileging of the gestural mode over the verbal serves to reproduce existing linguistic hierarchies which were pervasive in Turkish complementary school classrooms as well as among many members of the UK Turkish-speaking diaspora. In this example, the teacher and pupil privilege the use of the standard Turkish word *tükenmez* over the Cypriot-Turkish equivalent *penna* for <pen>. These linguistic hierarchies are rooted in the marginalised position of Cypriot-Turkish and the stigmatisation of regional varieties of Turkish, particularly regional accents, with respect to standard Turkish (Lytra and Baraç, 2008).

Nevertheless, it is important to acknowledge that Cypriot-Turkish was spoken widely by many of the pupils, teachers, parents and school administrators at home and across Turkish complementary school settings. These observations concurred with reports of high language maintenance and language loyalty among Londoners of Turkish-Cypriot heritage (Issa, 2008). By focusing on the intersection of the multilingual and multimodal we can further explore some of the tensions and contradictions which pupils and teachers in complementary school classrooms face between their actual language use and what was widely regarded as *temiz Türkçe* <clean, uncontaminated or standard Turkish>.

The focus on the intersection of the multilingual and the multimodal in instances of the official, vertical classroom discourse has provided us with a useful point of entry into the reproduction of key aspects of the local interactional order of Turkish and Gujarati classrooms. We observed that this local interactional order was jointly constructed by teachers and pupils but also that tensions and contradictions often arose. One fruitful avenue of further research would be to focus on those tensions and contradictions within classroom discourse in order to explore the participants' power relations, agency and unequal access to linguistic and other semiotic resources.

As we have discussed elsewhere (Lytra and Martin, 2009), the co-existence of semiotic resources, practices, discourses and genres that may be incongruent with each other is a permanent fixture of complementary school classrooms (but also mainstream classrooms, see Maybin, 2007). This is felt to be particularly strong in complementary school classrooms where aspects of the heritage language(s) and culture(s) may be at odds with aspects of the pupils' linguistic and cultural resources and forms of knowledge from other learning and out-of-school recreational contexts. A focus on the participants' multilingual and multimodal resources can show us how participants accommodate resources, practices, discourse and genres from outside the classroom within the official vertical classroom discourse.

## Acknowledgements

We thank the teachers and pupils from the Turkish and Gujarati complementary schools for kindly opening up their schools and classrooms to us. Also, a warm thanks to Kate Pahl for insightful comments on earlier drafts.

# 3

# Literacy and socialisational teaching in Chinese complementary schools

*Li Wei and Chao-Jung Wu*

## Introduction

The teaching of Chinese as a heritage language is a world-wide phenomenon, as studies in He and Xiao (2008) show. Chinese diasporic communities in all parts of the world have long been setting up schools and classes for their children. These schools and classes have a strong cultural flavour: they offer a variety of teaching that is associated with traditional Chinese cultural practices, such as martial arts, folk dancing, paper folding and cutting, calligraphy and ink painting. They also provide an important social network for Chinese diasporic communities where valuable information is being exchanged (eg information about school admission procedures for the children, university and career opportunities and other services) between families who otherwise are dispersed (see also Taylor, 1987; Tsow, 1980, 1983; Verma *et al*, 1999). However, the primary aim of these schools and classes is to teach literacy to the next generation of overseas Chinese children.

The Chinese language has unique linguistic features with regard to the writing system. The pictographic characters make it harder to learn for the overseas Chinese children who typically are exposed to alphabetic languages through their mainstream schooling. The Chinese people traditionally hold a strong belief that their writing system has a rich cultural heritage. Indeed, language teachers in China routinely spend a considerable amount of classroom time on the origin of Chinese written characters, which inevitably entails the retelling of folk tales.

In this chapter, we examine the activity of literacy teaching in the Chinese complementary schools context. We draw examples from our study of multilingual practices in Chinese complementary schools in Manchester, UK. These schools are voluntary organisations, set up by the Chinese communities to teach literacy to Chinese children, most of who are born in Britain. They take place over the weekend and focus exclusively on Chinese language and culture. They, therefore, complement the mainstream schooling the children receive during the week. Elsewhere, we have examined the pupils' creative use of multilingual resources and the tensions between ideology and practice in these schools (Li Wei and Wu, 2008, 2009). In the present chapter, we will show that the teaching of literacy in this particular context is not restricted to the teaching of Chinese written characters, but in fact involves a range of cultural activities. In unpacking what we call 'socialisational teaching' of literacy, ie impressing socio-cultural traditions and values on pupils through what seem to be mundane pedagogical activities in the Chinese complementary schools context, we wish to demonstrate the competing notions of culture and heritage between the school and the parent generation on the one hand and the British-Chinese children and youth on the other (cf. Creese *et al*, 2007; Jia, 2008; Wu, 2001, Francis *et al*, 2009, also Blackledge and Creese and Francis *et al* this volume). In doing so, we are contributing to the wider debate over heritage and the perceived loss of traditional culture and cultural values amongst immigrant communities (cf. Blackledge and Creese, 2008; Block, 2008).

## The study

As part of a large scale, comparative, team ethnographic study of multilingual practices in complementary schools of the Bengali, Gujarati, Turkish and Chinese communities in the UK we undertook an in-depth study of two Chinese complementary schools in Manchester, one Cantonese (NW) and one Mandarin (HX). Over a period of ten weeks, we made extensive observations, field notes, and audio and video recordings of all the activities during the school hours. We also conducted interviews with teachers, parents and the pupils. Like most Chinese complementary schools, the two schools we studied are set up by the communities themselves. They run language classes as well as martial arts, dancing, painting and calligraphy classes and other activities on Sunday afternoons for three or four hours.

NW is a well established school, which was set up in the 1970s. It has a direct link with the local Chinese association, which provides staff, resources and financial help. Many teachers (40 in all) are long-term residents in the local area, working in catering or other private businesses. The school had around 350 students at the time of our study, although the number had apparently fallen from 600 pupils in 1989 (Liao, 1992). Some pupils travel considerable distances to attend the school. Approximately 70 per cent of the pupils have connections with Hong Kong and 30 per cent with mainland China (Cantonese-speaking regions). Classes range from kindergarten through to Year 6. Each level is further divided into two or three groups. There is also a GCSE class and a Mandarin Chinese class. The school uses textbooks published by Ji Nan University in China, donated by the Chinese consulate in Manchester. The textbooks are designed especially for overseas Chinese and originally targeted the Chinese communities in North America.

HX is a relatively new establishment, set up in 1996. It has 180 pupils and 18 teaching and support staff including teachers for martial arts, dance, calligraphy and painting. Most of the teachers are mature postgraduate students at universities in Manchester; some are professionals such as lawyers, accountants and computer engineers. The pupils are all from middle-class families, whose parents are university educated. Classes run from Level 1 through to Level 7. There is high take-up for GCSE, AS, and A-level examinations. The school uses textbooks published by the People's Education Press of China. These have simplified written characters as well as pingyin, the Romanisation system to assist the teaching of pronunciation. The school has a resource centre for GCSE and AS- and A-level materials, and teachers often prepare supplementary materials. There is an adult language class on offer to non-Chinese and Cantonese speakers who wish to learn Mandarin. All the language teaching staff are women.

## Belief in the significance of literacy as cultural heritage

One of the clearest messages conveyed to us during our fieldwork in the two Chinese schools was the significance parents, teachers and pupils attached to literacy. And it was not simply the fact that Chinese writing was deemed to be difficult to learn and required serious teaching and learning. There was a widely held view that literacy in Chinese was a cultural symbol, a symbol of a long-lasting cultural heritage and of a cultured Chinese identity. The following extract is taken from an interview with one of the pupils whom we observed and recorded closely.

### Example 1

I: 你为什么会想学中文呢？

&lt;Why would you like to learn Chinese?&gt;

P: 因为我是中国人。

<Because I am Chinese (person)>

I: 你想学中文学到什么程度呢？

<What would you like to achieve in learning Chinese?>

P: 你想学中文学到什么程度呢？

<To be able to read and write.>

(interview with child, 01-10-06)

This is a sentiment frequently expressed by the young people attending Chinese complementary schools. They regard being able to understand, speak, read and write Chinese as an important symbol of being Chinese. Similarly, the teachers also regard Chinese language ability as crucial to being Chinese, as the following extract from a teacher interview illustrates.

**Example 2**

T: 其實我覺得在這裡長大的小朋友們...這是一個地方把這些小朋友們聚在一起。然後他們學到他們家鄉，他們這些，屬於華人的語言。

<In fact, I think for kids growing up here ... this (the school) is a place for them to gather together, to learn about their homeland ... their language, which belongs to the Chinese people.>

I: 像您自己編課程，您會帶一些歷史地理、文化的課程嗎？

<In your own curriculum, would you bring in elements of history, geography or culture?>

T: 也有的，我們課程裏面呢，我們選那個比較就是，可以看到

... (T looks through the textbook)...

比如説，這裡講的中國以前舊的文化。還有中國的一些

... (turning pages)

中外的名人。還有，以前又講一些像司馬光的。

<Yes, in our curriculum we choose those ... you can see ... For example, it talks about the old Chinese culture, and some of the Chinese ... famous people in China and from other countries. Also, we talked about Sima Guang before ... >

...

I: 您覺得中文學校就是提供他們一個學習的環境 ⋯

<You think Chinese school provides them an environment for learning ... >

T: 對，因爲我覺得…中國人嘛，就是一定要聽得懂、看得懂自己的文字…不論
這是廣東話，國語啊也好。

<Yes, I think ... Chinese people must be able to understand and read their own
language ... whether Cantonese or Mandarin.>

...

I: 這裡有華人社區，您在這裡教書，對您而言有什麼意義？

<Here's a Chinese community. What does it mean to you to teach here?>

T: 我覺得這是一個機會，把中國的文化傳給在海外土生土長的下一代。就是
沒有我們…沒有這個…他們就變成一個…不會講中文…但是一看卻是中國
人…然後，比如說他們去中國，向人問路…他卻聽不懂、看不懂中文。這
個是…覺得有一點…尷尬。

<I think this is an opportunity to transmit Chinese culture to the next generation who
are born and bred in this country. Without us ... without this ... they'd become ... not
able to speak Chinese. But look like a Chinese person. ... And for example if they
go to China and ask people for directions, if they cannot understand what they hear
or cannot read Chinese language, it feels a bit ... embarrassing.>

(interview with Cantonese class teacher, 25-06-06)

What is also remarkable about the teacher's response in this extract is his view
of the interrelationship between language and culture. It is a view that is
commonly expressed by all teachers and many parents. Understanding language as culture is a theme also discussed by Francis *et al* (2009) and in
Chapter 7.

## Socialisational teaching of literacy

In our observation in the two schools, we found that the teachers routinely
tried to relate the teaching of specific linguistic structures to some broader
socio-cultural issues. For example, the following field notes were made
during our observation of a class where the teacher was teaching the modal
verb should/must. But the examples she chose in teaching it were all related
to moral duties and behavioural norms, including respect and working hard.
What might have been a fairly basic grammatical drill is transformed into a
socialisation process.

## Example 3

The class teacher asked a boy to read out the sample sentence. Then she
asked them what the word 应该 <should, must> meant. After a short pause,
a girl answered (in English) 'must'. The teacher then asked pupils to make

sentences using the word. Pupils made sentences such as 我们应该尊敬长辈。 <we must respect members of the older generation>, 我们今年应该回中国。 <we must go back to China this year> ... Other sentences were offered. <you must study hard>, ' 你应该好好学习。<younger brother must have a good sleep>, 我应该做作业了。<I must do homework>.

In Example 4, the teacher is teaching the phrase *panwang* (longing for). But the examples she gives in collocation with panwang all concern higher socio-cultural ideals, such as having a united homeland and a united family.

**Example 4** (T: teacher, P(s): unidentified pupil(s), B: girl, L: boy)

T:   盼望。盼望怎么说？比如说，我们都盼望什么？盼望, *expect, look forward to. Write down the explanation beside the words, in case you forget it later.* 盼望, *the 4th one, means look forward to.* 比如说，我们都盼望什么？

    <Panwang (longing for). How do you use panwang? For example, what do we long for? panwang expect, look forward to. Write down the explanation beside the words, in case you forget it later. Panwang, the fourth one, means look forward to. For example, what do we panwang?>

P1: 时节.

    <Having festivals.>

P2: 圣诞节。

    <Christmas>

T:   世界杯？

    <the World Cup?>

P3: *No.*

P4: 吃月饼。

    <Eating mooncakes>

T:   我们都盼望吃月饼？ *Sounds a little strange.*

    <We all long for eating mooncakes? Sounds a little strange>

B:   *Birthday! My birthday!*

T:   我们都盼望着过圣诞节。白盼望着过生日。盼望 *can be a little big for all these occasions. get reunited.*

    比如说，我们都盼望着祖国统一，对吧？我们都盼望着祖国
    <We all long for Christmas. B longs for her birthday. Panwang can be a little big for all these occasions. For example, we all long for our mother country to get reunited, right? We all long for our mother country to get reunited>

L: 盼望中文学校完了。

<Long for Chinese school to finish.>
(students laugh)

T: 刘, *be serious*, OK?

<L, *be serious*, OK?>

L: *I am serious, I'm looking forward to it.*

T: 比如说，我们都盼望家人团聚。<For example, we long for family reunion>. *For example, if you are here in Manchester, your parents are back in China, and you have been separated for years, you are looking forward to the reunion of the family.*

S: 盼望天气…

<long for weather ... >

(classroom recording, 11-06-06)

It was clear from our interviews with the teachers and parents that this kind of socialisational teaching is exactly what the majority of them expected to happen in the Chinese complementary schools context. They do not see the school as the provider for narrowly defined language teaching. Instead, they want the school to offer a much broader education to the children and socialise them into a new generation of cultured Chinese. The following quote is from the Head Teacher of HX School which highlights the point:

**Example 5**

我们实际上强调的就是中文作为一种语言，语言作为一种文化载体，它有一些文化上的讯息，…

< We are in fact stressing Chinese as a language, language as a culture carrier. It contains cultural messages. ... >

(interview with head teacher, 15-10-06)

There is a strong sense that language teaching needs to be closely related to the transmission of cultural values, a sense that has been observed also by other researchers working on Chinese complementary schools in different parts of the world. In writing about her own experience learning literacy at a Canadian Chinese school, Curdt-Christiansen (2008) remarks on her observation that the teaching material always uses stories, folk tales, fables and other genres for teaching moral and cultural values:

Consequently, children learn written language through the reading of texts that explicitly teach them culturally appropriate values and socially accepted norms.

> Chinese textbooks tend to contain many of the culturally valued didactics, such as perseverance, filial piety, diligence, obedience, education and to give emphasis to the importance of effort, achievement, patriotism, etc. (p99)

Similarly, He (2000, 2008) details the discourse processes via which learners are socialised to values of respect for authority and group conformity through participating in these language classes.

## Challenging socialisational teaching

Whilst the parents and teachers clearly see a purpose in what we call socialisational teaching, ie teaching cultural values through language teaching, the pupils who are on the receiving end often challenge both the content and the manner in which they are taught. Space limitations prevent us from further exploring the notion of culture at a theoretical level. It seems clear from the following examples that the teachers and pupils have different ideas about China and Chinese cultural heritage.

In Example 6, the class teacher wants the pupils to write down the names of the Chinese historical dynasties. She has made them into a poem to aid memorisation. However, the pupils cannot see the point of learning the names and the sequence of the dynasties in the first place. Although they seem to be able to follow the proceedings of the class well and are engaged in the lesson, they feel that the task is too hard and pointless. In the first half of the example, they merely talk amongst themselves and make various comments in English, but not directly challenging the teacher. It is only when the teacher tries to stop them from talking that B1 begins to challenge the teacher, first with a question on why so many dynasties, followed by a sarcastic comment 'demolished, killed, eaten', which signals an end of the dynasties as well as his hope to finish the task. The teacher focuses on the task and continues to explain what happened after the Chinese imperial era came to an end. It is at this point that B1 asks the teacher, very boldly, to 'speak our language', ie English.

**Example 6** (T: teacher, B1, 2, 4: all boys, S1: unidentified pupil)

T: 那么中国的朝代啊，可以这样来记。它是一个 (shifting the boards)
诗歌的形式。有兴趣的同学，可以抄下去，最好抄下去。
<Chinese Dynasties, you can remember them this way. It's in a (shifting the boards) form of a poem. Those who are interested can copy it down, it's best that you do> (Teacher shifted the whiteboards while students talked a little)

B1: *Oh dear God!*

S1: *What's this?*

B1: *Something to do with.*

T: 朝代.

<Dynasty>

B1: *Yes.*

S1: *Oh God!*

T: 就通过记住这个，就知道所有中国的朝代了。谁在前，谁在后。

<If you memorise these, you'd know all the dynasties in China. Which one was first, which one followed>

B1: *We could not go back.*

B2: *You could do.*

B1: *Yeah. I'd like slaughter a XXX, they won't be like this hard.*
(students talk among themselves)

...

T: 别讲话了！赶快抄。

<Stop talking! Copy it down quickly.>

B: I can't (XXX) write down, just (XXX) 朝代歌<Song of Dynasties>?

...

B1: How come there were so many朝代 <dynasties>? Why say
一朝代，两朝代 <one dynasty, two dynasties> what the hell.
(Students copy and talk among themselves. Then there were questions about
how to write specific characters. T also read out what was written on the board.)

T: 怎么了？

<What's the matter>?

B1: *Demolished, killed, eaten.*

T: 王朝到此完，结束了。到清朝以后，就没有皇朝了，是不是？清朝以后就
是民国，然后中华人民共和国。

<That's the end of emperor era, all ended. There were no more emperors after
the Qing Dynasty, right? After the Qing Dynasty, there was the Republic of China,
and then the People's Republic of China.>

B1: *What? In English. Speak our language, man.*

B2: (XXX).

B4: *Never mind.*

(classroom recording, 18-06-06)

Example 7 comes from a Cantonese class where the teacher is trying to teach numerals in the traditional Chinese written characters rather than the Arabic numbers. The pupils, who are used to the latter cannot see the point of learning the Chinese characters and contest the way they are being taught. One pupil, Y, explicitly says: 'but we don't use them now.'

**Example 7** (T: teacher, G/P: unidentified pupil, H: male, Y: female)

T: 嗱,改好正的那些拿出堂課簿，抄黑板的字。

<u>\<Nah, those who finished the corrections, take out your exercise book and copy the characters on the blackboard\></u>

G: (moaning) *Oooh ... what for?*

T: 第一個是壹字，第二個是貳字，這些是中國的數字。

<u>\<The first character is the word 'one', the second is the word 'two', these are Chinese number words\></u>

P: (confirming understanding) 哦。

<u>\<Oh.\></u>

T: 壹是代表一，貳是代表二，叁是代表三，肆是代表四。

<u>\< 'one' represents 'one', 'two' represents 'two', 'three' represents 'three', 'four' represents 'four'\></u>

H: 喺堂課簿。

<u>\<In the exercise book\></u>

T: 是啦，在堂課簿。

<u>\<Yes, in the exercise book\></u>

G: (sighs) 唉。

<u>\<Ai.\></u>

T: 壹至拾。不是一至十次。壹是代表一的 '一' 字。是中國的文字。中國的數字一是這樣寫…

<u>\<'one' to 'ten', not one to ten times. 'One' represents 'one'. These are Chinese characters. Chinese number words are written like these ... \></u>

T: 這些是以前中國用的壹字。

<u>\<This is the word 'One' which used to be used in China\></u>

42

Y:  但我們現在不用。

<u>＜But we don't use them now＞</u>

T:  現在不用，但比你們認識一下，因爲有時會在報章上看到。所以給你們認識，這個是壹、貳、叁、肆、伍、陸、柒、玖、玖、拾。快點抄到堂課簿上。因爲在報紙上，有時你們會見到這些字。

<u>＜Not being used now, but just to let you know these. Sometimes you'll see them in the newspaper or magazine articles. Hence, (I'm) letting you know these. This is 'One', 'Two', 'Three', 'Four', 'Five', 'Six', 'Seven', 'Eight', 'Nine', 'Ten'. Copy them into your exercise book quickly. Because you'll sometimes see these words in newspapers＞</u>

(classroom recording, 02-07-06)

## Conclusion

The examples we have seen in this chapter illustrate a number of dimensions of literacy teaching in the Chinese complementary schools context. What we have chosen to focus on is its socialisational dimension. Almost all Chinese complementary schools across the world have a mission to teach literacy, as they strongly believe that the reading and writing of Chinese characters is an essential part of Chinese linguistic knowledge. What transpires though is the fact that the parents, teachers and pupils alike hold a belief that an ability to read and write Chinese characters is also an integral part of being Chinese. This complex association between language, especially literacy, and Chinese identity may have prompted the teachers to embed language teaching in cultural socialisation. In addition to the emphasis on correctly copying the characters, the teachers incorporate a significant amount of cultural knowledge in their teaching, either through their choice of examples or through the use of historical narratives and facts.

At the same time, we have seen that the pupils resist this kind of socialisational teaching by posing challenging questions to the teachers and making fun of the classroom activities. For them, China is a fast changing nation and an increasing world power, and not something that exists in the past, in old folk tales, archeological artifacts or in textbooks. On an everyday basis, we see the pupils listening to Chinese pop songs, reading Chinese comics and youth magazines and playing various card and computer games. Many of these activities require the ability to read Chinese characters. Yet, none of what the young British-Chinese seem to be interested in is reflected in the teaching in the Chinese complementary schools. For the schools, the teachers and the parents, the emphasis seems to be on a rather static notion of Chinese cultural heritage that lasted for a very long time and exists only in print. The pupils, however, seem to think of themselves primarily as British youths of Chinese heritage. While accepting literacy as being an important part of being Chinese, they reject the simplistic association of Chinese culture soley with the past.

Chinese complementary schools as world-wide socio-educational institutions have played a major role in the lives of thousands of Chinese diasporic families. Yet, there has been little critical reflection on the policies and practices in these schools. The Chinese complementary schools are an important site of multilingualism where different language ideologies, beliefs and practices are competing with each other. There is no doubt that through this competition new sets of diasporic cultural identities emerge, which have a long-lasting impact on the Chinese diasporic communities and the individuals of different generations. It is hoped that the discussion of the examples in this chapter both contributes to the exploration of the multiple dimensions of this particular site of multilingualism and opens up further debate over the interculturality of diasporic communities.

## Acknowledgements

We gratefully acknowledge the support of the Economic and Social Research Council of Great Britain for the project 'Investigating multilingualism in complementary schools in four communities' (ESRC, RES-000-23-1180) from which this paper draws its examples.

*Transcription conventions*

| | |
|---|---|
| Mandarin Chinese translation | <Plain font> |
| Cantonese translation | <Plain font, underline> |
| English | *Italic* |
| ... | short pause |
| (plain font) | additional information |
| (XXX) | inaudible |

# 4

## *Abetare* and dancing: the story of a partnership

### *Raymonde Sneddon*

It is almost 5 o'clock on an evening in early November. There are lights on in school, but all is quiet. Mothers and children are arriving for the Albanian class. They sit on benches in the playground and chat in the gathering dusk while the children run around. The air is still mild. Ana arrives laden with bags full of teaching materials, the children come up to her and greet her with a hug. Trim, the dance teacher, arrives and the little group move in to the warmth of the mainstream school building. The door is left open for late-comers. The children say good bye to their mothers and follow both teachers into a classroom. The two hour session will be split with the younger children learning Albanian with Ana for the first hour while the older children learn dance steps and play games in the gym, then they will swap over.

## Introduction

This chapter tells the story of the partnership between a primary school that values the language and culture of its children and a community organisation that works with it to support the children's bilingualism and emerging identities. It follows the children as they move from a language class that uses *Abetare*, an Albanian teaching programme, to learning the complex steps of traditional dancing. In interviews with the researcher, they reflect on their experiences. The article is part of an ongoing two-year evaluative study that will map the developing partnership between *Shpresa*, the community organisation, and Gascoigne school and explore its impact on the attainment of children of Albanian heritage.

## The research and policy context

Of particular relevance to the formation of the partnership is the theoretical model developed by Cummins (1984, 1996, 2000). Through a concern for social justice, this model identified aspects of education that can seriously disable learners who speak minority languages in contexts in which they have no access to bilingual education. However, Cummins (1986, 1996) suggests that incorporating the language of the community into the school, even if it can't actually be taught, and involving families and the community in the education of the children can support educational achievement. He argues that building on pupils' cultural knowledge and language skills and providing teaching that 'affirms their identities and enables them to invest their identities in learning' leads to successful academic engagement (Cummins *et al*, 2006). It is just such a concern that led the school to engage with the Albanian organisation.

The work of Pavlenko and Blackledge on multidimensional identities (2004) and of Creese *et al* (2006) in complementary schools also shows how identity development can be supported through the interaction of language and culture in a safe space. Harris's study of bilingual pupils in west London demonstrates what pupils' own informal speech reveals about their developing identities (2006). Recent work on the development of multiliteracy by Gregory (2008, Gregory *et al*, 2004) and Kenner (2004), reveals children who not only cope, but thrive, on becoming literate in languages which may be taught in very different ways in different settings. The research shows how their experiences can lead them to a deeper understanding of how their languages work and to reflect on the relationship between their languages, as the children in the present study demonstrate. Community organisations can play a key role in supporting parents to engage more successfully with their children's schools (Sneddon, 1997) and support the school in making better use of parents' 'funds of knowledge' and expertise (Gonzalez *et al*, 1993, see also Barradas this volume).

While the lack of status and support for community languages in the UK has been well documented (Conteh *et al*, 2007), the Department for Children, Schools and Families (DCSF) has recently expressed an interest in the teaching of community languages (DfES, 2002) and acknowledged the value of complementary education. This has led to the funding of the *Our Languages* project to encourage the teaching of community languages through partnerships between complementary and mainstream schools (CILT, 2008a). The model suggested reflects what Shpresa had already initiated in east London and the organisation was invited to submit a case study as an example of good practice in partnership (CILT, 2008b).

## The context of the partnership

Gascoigne Primary School was built in the 1970s near the commercial centre of a borough which, until their recent downsizing, provided the labour force for the enormous Ford factories near the river Thames. The school is sur- rounded by small Victorian houses and both low and high rise council hous- ing. From being an almost exclusively white working class neighbourhood, the area is now very ethnically mixed. It is not, however, economically mixed. Unemployment is high, leading to high levels of deprivation and to political tensions in the community. In Gascoigne School, 88 per cent of children are learners of English as an additional language, 25 per cent have refugee status and 50 per cent are entitled to free school meals.

The school is 'a haven of calm within the community'. The report by Ofsted, the body that inspects schools, describes it thus and elaborates: 'pupils ... enjoy school and appreciate the wide range of additional activities provided for them. Pupils' spiritual, moral, social and cultural development is out- standing, and a tribute to the school's very good pastoral care and support' (Ofsted, 2007:1).

One of these additional activities has been run by *Shpresa* (meaning hope in Albanian) since September 2007. The organisation was set up to meet the needs of the community of Albanian speakers living in east London, many of whom arrived from the mid-1990s as asylum seekers (Sneddon and Martin, 2008). *Shpresa* organises Albanian classes and a range of dance, drama, sport- ing and cultural activities for children and young people in after-school, weekend and holiday programmes. The organisation has developed a power- ful model of partnership with mainstream schools, running classes in six boroughs in north and east London. In return for the free use of premises, it offers activities for children, information about language and culture, sup- ports teachers and parents to establish relationships and can also set up workshops for women to enable them better to support their children's edu- cation and get involved in the life of the school. *Shpresa* also raises the profile of Albanian culture through organising performances of Albanian dance by the children, both in school and in public venues.

When *Shpresa* approached the school to offer its services to the 100 Albanian speaking children on roll, the headteacher was cautious: 'I was very wary in the beginning because I had worked with lots of parents' groups in the past.

The idea is always very good, I am very positive, but it can mean an awful lot of work for the school' (CILT, 2008b). He agreed to work in partnership with *Shpresa* for a trial period of three months and, realising how thoroughly professional and competent the organisation was, became enthusiastic about the benefits of the partnership.

### *Abetare* in the classroom

Back in the classroom, the children have hung up their coats and the older group has followed Trim to the gym. The younger children sit in horse-shoe formation around large tables facing the whiteboard. The arrangement is formal and reflects the style of teaching. The children have only an hour to learn basic literacy in Albanian. Ana tells the children: '*Tani do të prezamtojme veten tone. Gjithe secili do të thotë emrin e tij dhe sa vjeç është*' (Now we are going to introduce ourselves. Everyone has to say their name and how old they are). Antoneta stands up confidently: '*Unë jam Antoneta dhe jam 7 vjeç*' (My name is Antoneta and I am 7). The other children follow in turn. Ana asks them: '*çfarë date është sot?*' (what is today's date?). The children respond in unison: '*sot është 6 Nentor 2008*' (today is 6th November 2008).

All the children in this class started school speaking only Albanian, but all have now become dominant in English. In earlier interviews mothers have expressed great concern over their children's loss of fluency and confidence in Albanian. Ana is very aware of this and explains that, as well as teaching literacy and aspects of different subjects such as history, geography and maths, she is intent on getting the children to hear and respond to a good model of language:

She conducts the whole lesson in Albanian, mostly from the front of the class. She has a warm and expressive voice, articulates carefully and uses body language and props from her large bags.

Albanian uses the Roman alphabet and has a regular grapho-phonic relationship. There is a strong emphasis in this programme on learning the letters that represent the 36 phonemes of Albanian. An understanding of this relationship can help children to transfer their reading skills from English to Albanian with comparative ease (Sneddon, 2008).

Ana distributes flash cards for the children to use in pairs and follows this with illustrated letter cards attached to the whiteboard: Aa for *ariu* (a bear), Rr for *rosa* (a duck), Ee for *elefant* (an elephant) and Eë for *ëmbelsira* (a cake). The children know exactly what is expected of them, they respond rapidly, individually or in unison; Ana builds up the pace *spejt! spejt!* (quick); the atmosphere becomes competitive. The lesson then moves on to the initial letters of children's names. Ana explains the difference between consonants (*bashkëtingël-lore*) and vowels (*zanore*). The children count the letters and digraphs from an alphabet chart (36), consonants (29) and vowels (7). They move on to blending single sounds into syllables.

Ana hands out individual exercise books that are part of the *Abetare* literacy scheme and explains the tasks. The page they are using focuses on the letter I (pronounced 'ee' in Albanian). It includes handwriting practice, completing words, and a simple dictation exercise. Some children are working individually in their books, individuals come out to the board and make up short words with letter cards. One demonstrates *'unë – Ina – jam'* (My name is Ina). Another reads: *Unë jam Iliri, Ilda, Indrit*. The class chant what is on the board.

The lesson moves on. Rebeca volunteers a well known poem about the Albanian national Flag Day:

> *Babanë epyeti Beni*
> *O babi a e di?*
> *Pse flamurin e kemi?*
> *Dy ngjyrqsh kug e zi? ...*

(Beni asked his father 'father, do you know why our flag has the colours black and red?') She recites two stanzas; Ana supports her with a couple of prompts and all the children clap. Another child recites another section in a quiet voice and is also cheered.

The only real opportunity for children to use spontaneous language is when Ana asks them to talk about the half-term holiday which they had the week before. A boy stands up and starts 'Last week I ... ' Ana interrupts 'In Albanian!' He continues in Albanian to tell the class that he played in a football match and that his team won. Saima comments: 'excellent!' On this occasion he is the only one to rise to the challenge of describing holiday activities in Albanian.

Towards the end of the session Ana summarises the lesson, reminding the children what they have learned. She moves them onto the mat and leads a game. She calls out: *'vigani!'* (tall) and *'skkurtabiqi!'* (small). The children respond by standing or crouching. The children are playing a kind of Simon Says game. The leader stands or squats and calls out an instruction. She tries to confuse them by doing the wrong action: the children must do what she says, not what she does. The pace is fast. Ana encourages the children to take on the role of leader of the game. They do, and loudly. A few children are talking excitedly in Albanian. The children are enjoying the game and they cheer and clap. Ana tells them it is time to pack up their workbooks and go to the gym for their dance lesson. They cheer again.

The *Abetare* programme that Ana is using is geared to teaching children in Albania. It includes a wide range of resources including stories and audio materials as well as textbooks and workbooks, some of which the children use at home. She differentiates lessons for the individual children in the class, taking account of their varying skills in Albanian and ensuring they hear a good model of speech. Although Ana has reported that she uses English if it is necessary to ensure understanding, there is little evidence of this in the lesson. There is also very little evidence of the children using a mixed code as reported, for example, in Gujarati classes in Leicester (Creese and Martin, 2006). The children have been speaking entirely in Albanian throughout this class, but because of the way in which the class is run and the time constraints, there is little opportunity for them to speak among themselves. However, the pace is fast and lively and it keeps the children very focused.

## Dancing

While the *Abertare* is taught in the classroom, dancing and games are going on, first with the older children, then with the younger. The gym is bright and spacious. On benches round the side two mothers are sitting, watching and chatting. They live too far away to go home and come back for their children.

The older children are in a circle. Trim speaks in English: 'OK, you know the words?' They children are playing a statues game. Two children chase the others. When the leader calls '*ngriva!*' those who manage to freeze instantly cannot be caught. When the leader calls '*shriva!*' the players un-freeze and they are chased again. The children are very excited and running and shouting in both Albanian and English.

Trim sits the children down in a circle to reflect on their learning:

Trim:        We're going to play that again soon. Now, can you tell me why we play this game? Come on.

Child:      To learn words?

Trim:        OK, so we learn words. What else?

Child:      To work as a team.

Trim:        Perfect! To work as a team. Because there were two people working together, then the rest. So we had to work as one team and they had to work as one team. That is quite good. That's important in the dancing too, working as a team. Because you are altogether dancing, and one of you, in the middle of the dance, as she is doing now, is doing something different. So it changes the team. OK? So if you be as a team, you can make it work. Yeah?

50

What do you think? So did you all work as a team? You didn't plan anything. Me with her (the girl who was his partner) we planned. Him and her, they planned ... So you can help each other. OK? Good. OK. So what is next? OK? You tell me. So why is that game?

Child: To work in pairs and get exercise.

Trim: Exercise. Always, everywhere you go, exercise is in everything you do. Dancing is exercise. As you learn you work as a team. Why is working as a team so important?

Child: To make it work.

Trim: What we are going to do is, I want you in one line first.

The children line up, try to pair up, hesitate, get confused, shriek with laughter. They play a game which involves responding rapidly to the number they have been given. The pace is very fast and the children are challenged when it gets faster still.

After the games the children move into a dance formation, in two lines facing the teacher, girls in front, boys behind. Trim demonstrates the steps and counts '1, 2, 3, 4, 5, 6, 7, 8' to keep the rhythm. The children are watching carefully and are very intent on getting the steps right. 'Sometimes you have to do this on a big stage or a small stage. Sometimes you are going to have a big hall, sometimes a small one. So you have to get used, OK.?' Trim demonstrates two different formations: with children spread out or closer together. He counts to keep the beat and the pace gets faster and faster. Children are concentrating hard and following his lead very closely. The steps are getting ever more complicated. All of this practice is without music. The CD player on the bench is not used.

Next, Trim arranges the children in a triangular formation. This is difficult and Trim is moving children around to get them in the right position: 'If you stay behind her, it's an issue. You're hiding. So always stay on her right side. OK? So it's a triangle, so another girl should be there which she's not. Yep. OK. So this is your place. Ready? Let's go. 1, 2, 3, 4, 5, 6, 7 other side. 1, 2, 3, 4, 5, 6, 7 and again.' He keeps counting and setting up the elaborate dance pattern, occasionally repositioning the children. 'Me and her go back, and them two and you are going to go forward. OK? We're going to go. 1, 2, 3, 4, 5, 6, 7, 8, so you come her.' It is a very intricate dance and the tempo is speeding up.

Later the younger children go to the gym. This time Trim starts with dancing. They are practising very complex patterns with fierce concentration and are really working well in time and keeping the rhythm. The teacher tells the children 'if you do the dance good, we can play games'. He moves on to the same games played with the older children. The children are excited but remain disciplined and laugh a lot when they make mistakes.

Trim has chosen to speak in English with the children, using Albanian only when it was an integral part of the game. He is engaging the children in reflection and teaching co-operation and team-work. He has high expectations of the children and they respond with team-work and discipline. The results are remarkable; it is obvious why the public performances of the children are popular.

## Back in the classroom

When the older children come in from their dancing lesson they settle down to a board game. *Zhongleri* (juggler) encourages the children to use new vocabulary to describe pictures.

Like the younger children, they spoke Albanian when they started school and are now dominant in English.

The boards are packed away. The Albanian national day is in three weeks' time (28th November) and this is the opportunity for a history lesson. Ana is talking entirely in Albanian, but slowly, with expression, using body language, pictures, maps and artefacts. She is asking questions and the children are responding in Albanian, much more confidently than the younger children. The lesson works well as a language lesson: I only know a few words of Albanian, but I can follow it and learn about Albanian heroes, Ismail Qemali, Mother Theresa, and the significance of the *flamuri* (the flag). I learn from the map about the greater Albania and understand that it was broken up at a conference in 1913.

Ana hands out a page of text about the flag day and asks the children to underline words they don't know as she reads the text. Children ask for explanations and then take turns at reading. Ana nods approval and encouragement and then makes one of her rare statements in English. 'Next week we are going to do this. We are going to do a concert about this, because 28 November is our flag day. That's why I am doing something. OK?' She writes questions on the board and uses the opportunity to focus children on questioning words like *kur* (when) and *kush* (who).

The history lesson ends with an enthusiastic and rousing rendition of the 'flag song'. The children know most of the words, but Ana is intent on ensuring they are all word perfect for a performance and hands out a printed copy. Her last words to the class are in English: 'Next week we're going to do it again, but you have to learn at home, with your mum and with your dad, OK?' The caretaker comes in and starts checking the windows, Ana and the children rush to tidy, stuff their homework in their bags and grab their coats. A group of mothers and fathers are waiting for them in the hall and they disperse into the dark and the cold outside as the caretaker locks up at precisely 7 o'clock.

## Children's voices

The observations have shown children working seriously and enjoying the different aspects of their Albanian space. In recorded discussions with the researcher they articulate their feelings about bilingualism, about cultural confidence, about their mainstream school and the Albanian class. The children give the matter deep thought and have a great deal to say. Four boys and four girls, aged from 8 to 12, who attend the Albanian classes were interviewed in pairs. The following section includes some key responses.

When asked 'some people think that speaking two languages makes you clever. How do you feel about being bilingual?', Claudine (aged 10) explains 'I quite like being, speaking two languages because it makes you quite different and you stand out from the rest, and I'm trying to go for French as well'. Vanessa explains that she feels 'quite special. Because some people only speak English and they want to try and speak other languages but they can't, like, do the accent, and they can't really pronounce it properly'. Both girls report teachers showing an interest in Albanian and asking children to teach them some words.

Edi, who has just started secondary school, is in no doubt about the benefits of multilingualism: 'There's, like, lots of people that know more than one language that are in the top set. I'm in the top set for all my subjects'. He is learning French and has been invited to join the Latin class. 'If you know more than one language, if you have a job that you have to go abroad it will be easier for you to communicate with people' and with respect to Albanian in particular he comments 'it's important to learn and speak and write your own language. You might have to go back to your own country and, if you haven't learned it, like, it would be hard for you to adjust'.

Lala (aged 8) has found that people in school are impressed and 'they say we're clever'. Monica values her Albanian class 'because we get to learn how to write and ... you can learn two languages and it makes yourself clever'. She thinks there is another great advantage: she can have a secret conversation with her friends or her parents. Regarding switching between two languages, Arian is in no doubt that this is no problem: 'you just say it. Change straight away, like'. But Xhuli disagrees on this point and comments, 'it's difficult ... you can't learn two languages at the same time', but declines to elaborate.

The children appreciate their language class 'I think it's great', says Claudine, 'because it teaches you more Albanian that you don't actually understand that much. And it makes you learn more and then you can communicate with your family in Albania'. They express appreciation for the careful explanations and comment on the way their work is marked and how this helps them to progress.

The question 'do you think that learning Albanian helps or not with learning English?' prompts some deep thinking about how it feels to be living in two languages and two cultures and provides some insights into the children's awareness of their bilinguality. The children are very clear about the importance of English: 'English, you live in it, you have to speak it every single day'. Vanessa explains that you wouldn't understand anything in school if you weren't good at it.

Geni tells me 'I do think if you know two languages you can learn more stuff about two languages and you have to use your brain even more. Because you have two languages and you have two rules. Like two types of rules, the Albanian rules and English rules. And if one rules says, um, eat at night time and if the English rules says, um, eat lunch-time and eat breakfast at lunch, at night and the Albanian rules says eat lunch at day time. It will be a little bit complicated. Then, you have to do both of them at the same time. It's about the rules. A little bit complicated how you think about different things'.

Claudine explains the relationship between her languages: 'They're structured the same way but some of the sentences are, one word could be before the other one and it could still make sense in Albanian'.

While the children are appreciative of the opportunity to learn Albanian they become really animated when talking about dancing and performing. Edi and Monica were thrilled to be dancing and reciting poetry on stage with microphones. 'If we go on a concert', says Vanessa, 'it feels like you're going on TV and being, like, popular. My friends, like, say, 'I want to go to the concert, I want to do that!" Lala tells how, since coming to the classes, the very disciplined dancing 'came up in my brain and I know how to do it!' But there is more to dancing than just feeling like a television star. Vanessa and Claudine explain the cultural importance of being able to hold their own at community weddings. Weddings in Albania are very much focused around a large party with music, explains Claudine 'it's very important so you'll know how to dance in an Albanian wedding. You can't just stand still and think, what are they doing?' Vanessa and her friend went to her sister's wedding and 'me and her, we were practising a dance and we done it in front of the stage and everyone was clapping and cheering'.

## Discussion and conclusion

It is clear from the children's statements above that their language is acknowledged and valued in the school and that they have never been made to feel embarrassed about speaking another language at home. The school's awareness of the benefits of bilingualism and of the importance of incorporating language and culture in the curriculum led them to engage with *Shpresa*. The partnership provided the means to raise the children's skills in Albanian and enabled the whole school, through the performance of poetry and dance, to engage with Albanian culture. At this stage of the study it is not possible to say whether, as suggested by Cummins' empowerment model, the partnership has had an impact on the children's measured achievement in English. But the test data at the end of the first year of partnership suggests that the children's literacy skills are developing well and that they are catching up with the moving target of their peers.

I have focused here on the children's experiences of Albanian classes and the opportunities they are offered to explore their ethnicities in this safe space. The children's own voices reveal how they synthesise the Albanian and the English, the old with the new, in their everyday lives. The setting offers a range of spaces for exploring language and culture. The language class is very culturally Albanian: Albanian is mainly used with just a little English, the materials are imported, the teaching style, while lively, is traditional. The dance class provides almost the reverse: mainly English used by the teacher with a little Albanian. The children are using their new language while developing the very traditional skill of Albanian folk dancing.

While the children's observations reveal the importance to them of maintaining and developing their Albanian, the language they use to explain this, like that of the children studied by Harris (2006), is firmly anchored in the locality, in this case east London, and reveals the Britishness in their identity. Their observations in relation to folk dancing, wedding traditions and public performances shows the children synthesising the traditional dance and poetry of their Albanian heritage with the talent shows they enjoy watching on television and the opportunity offered to them to 'be famous'. The school's Ethnic Minority Achievement co-ordinator has noted the children's confidence in their developing identities: 'They talk about the club and the things that they have done and they really love going out to perform in other schools. The children talk about Albania, dancing, and their culture and wanting to fit in to the community here' (CILT, 2008b).

This chapter has considered the development of children's language and identity. Other aspects of *Shpresa's* input have resulted in a strong involvement of Albanian parents in the school as well as the provision of volunteers to work alongside teachers and to sit on the school's board of governors. The partnership continues to develop and has plans for the future. *Shpresa* is aware of the need to adapt the Albanian curriculum, the teaching style and language use to the needs of London children dominant in English and conducts regular training and review sessions for its teaching staff. The organisation is campaigning for a more formal recognition of the language in the form of examinations such as GCSE.

Both the headteacher and the director of *Shpresa* are keen to demonstrate the benefits that children derive from a positive and creative commitment to community cohesion and to develop and spread their model to other schools and other communities. As the headteacher explains:

> All I have got for them is praise. As a model of how things work, it's a very good model. I could convince other schools as well. All I get is really good pay-back for it, in community relations, parental relations and during an Ofsted inspection, for example. I am more than happy. There are no disadvantages (CILT, 2008b).

Note: *All children have chosen their pseudonyms. The headmaster requested that the school's real name be used. A fuller account of the initiative in the school appears in Sneddon 2009).*

# 5

## Grandmothers as orchestrators of early language and literacy lessons

*Mahera Ruby, Eve Gregory, Charmian Kenner*
*and Salman Al-Azami*

Five-year-old Nusrat lives with her parents, an older sister Israt and younger twin sisters in a block of flats in the East End of London. Aisha is the maternal grandmother of Nusrat and Israt. In 2003 Aisha came to London to support her daughter with her newborn twins. They live in Bromley-By-Bow, an ancient parish in the borough of Tower Hamlets. Two hundred years ago, it was a rural village with a pond and village green. A mixture of tower blocks sitting uneasily beside many Victorian houses has now replaced this rural idyll. The blocks appear very shabby in contrast with the glamorous Canary Wharf banking and business centre that sports a flashing pyramid and dominates the sky-line along the river to the South. The area also houses the historical building Kingsley Hall; its two most famous inhabitants were Mahatma Gandhi and RD Laing.

This area hosts a high percentage of Bangladeshi British families. In 2001, according to the UK national census data, 40 per cent of the population was of Bangladeshi origin, and this percentage has since increased. Most of the children in the area attend the two local primary schools. The local Muslim community has recently built a mosque, which many of the children attend for their Qur'anic and Bengali classes after school. Some families, however, choose not to send their children to the Mosque as it has a high pupil/teacher ratio. Nusrat's parents have decided to teach their daughters at home and their grandmother Aisha teaches them. Other children whose parents were keen for Aisha to teach them Qur'anic Arabic as well as Bangla very soon joined them. The classes take place in rotation between the three children's houses. Aisha is in her late forties and thoroughly enjoys her teaching. When asked about this she stresses that she is fulfilling a wider role than that of an average grandmother since she is helping these children to hold onto their culture, language and open a channel of communication with the older generation of their families by being able to speak the language as well as appreciate the culture. Aisha also mentions the generation gap she sees in and around the area, which she feels is mainly due to their language barrier.

## Introduction

This is a typical scenario both in Bangladesh and amongst the Bangladeshi British community: the grandmothers tend to take on the role of teacher to the children in the immediate family and the neighbourhood. Our aim in this chapter is to highlight this unique intergenerational relationship, which has hitherto been largely absent from research studies. We set out to investigate a pattern of learning which we refer to as 'orchestrated learning', where the grandmother's role bears similarities to that of a conductor of an orchestra. Like members of an orchestra, each child has a role to play and makes a contribution that is important to the learning events that occur. Within this context, we go on to explore the skill of the grandmother as a conductor of the young people with whom she works. As such, our grandmother's class shares the cultural and linguistic knowledge imparted in complementary classes. Additionally, however, we see here the relaxed atmosphere of a home, a smaller group than in the complementary classes and a more personal relationship between teacher and children. She can, therefore, bring the home and complementary school together in one site.

## Perspectives on learning in cross-cultural contexts

Our interpretation of the literacy event described below is grounded in theories focusing on the socio-historical, inter and intrapersonal nature of learning (Vygotsky, 1978). In other words, we draw upon studies that understand cognition to be intimately linked with the social and cultural context in which children learn and to be the result of a co-construction of meaning between the younger or less experienced and the older or more experienced participant in an activity. This interpretation is often referred to as viewing learning within a socio-cultural framework. However, the nature of co-construction and how it takes place has been the subject of a number of studies since the mid-twentieth century. Early work conducted by Wood, Bruner and Ross (1976) with young children completing a task alongside their caregivers referred to the adult's role as that of 'scaffolding' a child's learning through carefully controlled help which was then removed as the child grew confident with the task. Later studies criticised the overuse of this term on the grounds that it emphasised the role of the adult rather than the crucial participation of the child (Stone, 1993) and the western orientation of existing research, which marginalised non-western child rearing practices (Rogoff, 1990, 2003). Using observations of toddlers and their caregivers from seven countries, Rogoff and her colleagues introduced the term 'guided participation' to stress the active role of the child in learning (Rogoff *et al*, 1993). Like Dunn (1989), they proposed that, although caregivers from all cultural backgrounds give their infants finely-tuned guidance, the nature of the curriculum they provide is different.

Recent studies have provided further evidence for the special nature of teaching and learning in families that have moved to live in a new country. Our own work has investigated the learning taking place between siblings and grandparents of Bangladeshi British origin with young children. Here we refer to a release of 'synergy' where partners together achieve a task they could not complete alone. Thus, we show how older and younger siblings learn together as they play school (Gregory, 2001) and how grandparents and young children manage a task using computers through mutual teaching and learning (Kenner *et al*, 2008). The teaching and learning we describe in this chapter adds a further dimension to existing research in this field.

We use the term 'orchestrated learning' as an analogy, to illustrate the teaching and learning taking place between a grandmother and a group of young children learning the Bengali alphabet at home. Like the conductor of an orchestra, the grandmother invites each child to make a unique contribution; like members of an orchestra, the children listen, observe, imitate and lead the others in the group. The excerpts below detail ways in which this takes place in one home. The focus in this chapter is on the skill of the grandmother in facilitating the learning of the whole group rather than the children as members of the orchestra. To our knowledge the term 'orchestrated learning' has not been used in this way before.

## Background and methodology

Recent research (Kenner *et al*, 2004; Creese *et al*, 2006, 2008) has begun to show ways in which children from the second and third generation of families who have immigrated to the UK are involved in literacy learning activities within their communities. These studies reveal the safe spaces that exist within which the students can explore their identities in relation to their languages and cultures. Such spaces may be complementary classes, religious venues or children's homes. Our project *Developing bilingual learning strategies in mainstream and community contexts* (Kenner *et al*, 2004) aimed to uncover the bilingual learning taking place in some of these safe spaces and to build upon this knowledge in mainstream classroom practice. Our research involved small groups of children between the ages of 7 and 11, from second or third generation Bangladeshi British families who were mostly more fluent in English than in their mother tongue, as well as mainstream teachers and bilingual assistants from two primary schools. The findings from the small focus groups enabled the teachers to develop whole-class lessons involving bilingual strategies. The overall project provided an opportunity not only to enhance theoretical understanding of bilingual learning but also to ascertain whether and how cognitive and cultural benefits might apply to children who have been born and brought up in the UK, and how this affects their identities as learners.

The excerpts presented below form part of a larger bank of data collected through field-notes, digital video and audio-recording in children's complementary classes over one year. For the purpose of this chapter we focus on a class that we were able to video-record in a home close to the school which Nusrat (aged 5) and her sister Israt (aged 8) attended for Qur'anic as well as Bangla classes. Present at the session analysed below are Majid (aged 9), Nusrat, Israt and two toddlers. Majid and the two toddlers are siblings. All the children are from the immediate community. An interesting aspect of this particular class is that Aisha, who played the unique role of what we will refer to here as a conductor of an orchestra, is the maternal grandmother to these two sisters. As the researcher, Mahera Ruby was able to observe a lesson at home in which Aisha skilfully organised activities so that the children from toddlers to upper primary all participated in orchestrated learning involving reading, writing and speaking in Bengali.

Because of the complexity of the dynamics of this social group, Ruby spent rather longer getting to know the family and being accepted as part of the learning group. This enabled her to exercise a naturalistic approach within a project that was mainly Action Research. A naturalistic approach is a form of qualitative research, which Greig and Taylor (2002:47) describe as research where 'qualitative becomes non-experimental research which is subjective, insider, holistic, naturalistic, valid, inductive, exploratory, ungeneralisable, and discovery oriented'. As a Bangladeshi British person who had been born and partly raised in Bangladesh before moving to London, Ruby had little difficulty in taking an insider approach, since the whole event was very familiar to her own experiences. More problematic in some ways was the need to remain an outsider and faithful to the observations made. As

Hammersley and Atkinson (1993:9) state, 'even where he/she is researching a familiar group or setting, the participant observer is required to treat this as 'anthropologically strange', in an effort to make explicit presuppositions he/she takes for granted as a cultural member'. Ruby's position as insider/outsider and her heightened awareness of this contradiction helped Aisha who, on the one hand, felt very familiar and comfortable with the researcher's presence, yet on the other hand was happy to be seen as expert with Ruby in the role of novice or stranger. Aisha's ease helped the children to be natural and seemingly oblivious to the video-recording of the event which is examined below.

## The conductor and her orchestra: a synopsis of the performance

When the conductor of an orchestra makes their public appearance at a performance, it is not the beginning of their duties but more like the final moments of a long journey. So it is for Aisha. In her late forties, she came to the UK to visit her eldest daughter and ended up staying longer than expected to support her with her newborn twins. Before she took up the role of a teacher within the community, she had to build a relationship within her local community based on trust and respect, which was not always easy in an alien country and a culture she was unfamiliar with. However she was partly fortunate that her daughter lived in an area that is predominantly Bangladeshi although most of the community does not come from the same district as herself.

Aisha is from Noakhali, a small district in Bangladesh. Most of the families living in the East End of London are from Sylhet and speak the Sylheti dialect, which is very different from the Noakhali dialect. The Sylheti dialect is a variety of Bengali that no longer has a written version. Some families speak varieties other than Sylheti, and the term Bangla is used in the Tower Hamlets community to cover all varieties including Standard Bengali, which is used in books and newspapers, and spoken on TV. The Sylheti culture is also slightly different from the cultural practices of people from Noakhali. Again, due to this factor, Aisha needed to be accepted by the local community elders and youngsters alike before she was asked to take on this highly esteemed role of a teacher to their children.

Aisha herself had a very limited formal education. She completed her primary education in her local village school in Bangladesh. Her place in her own children's lives as a teacher shaped some of her learning as well as her teaching skills.

Regardless of the area of origin for the Bangladeshi families living in the borough, grandparents have a unique and common role. Grandparents are a generation that is revered by their immediate families as well as the surrounding community members. The parent generation seeks their wisdom and their companionship is sought after by the grandchildren's generation.

The following synopsis is a window into the session Ruby observed and which we examine below:

Aisha teaches the children Bangla once a week and Qur'anic Arabic for four days. On a heavy rainy day I made my way to Nusrat's house to find out that the class was going to take place in Majid's house that day, which was situated on the first floor of a very run down block of flats. The stairwells leading up to the flat were littered with cigarette butts and were wet from the rain. However, we were greeted very warmly by the host family and without many formalities Aisha made her way to the living room with the children while the mums all gathered in the kitchen. The flat was very spacious and brightly lit. The décor was a warm and comfortable welcome after the dreary entrance. The living room boasted expensive leather sofas, a large dining table as well as a wide screen plasma TV.

I sat with the children and Aisha in the living room around the dining table with the two toddlers (T1 and T2) both younger siblings of Majid hovering around the living room. I explained to them what I would be doing and the purpose behind the research. I took this opportunity to explain to them how the research would be used as well the fact that confidentiality would be maintained at all times. While Aisha settled them in their places at the table I set up the video equipment.

Aisha sat on one side of the dining table with Israt, Nusrat and Majid sitting opposite her across the table. The children did a number of activities within the session and the books used were from Bangladesh, which served the purposes of religious education as well as language and literacy learning. Once Aisha settled the children with their books, writing tools and exercise books she takes Nusrat's book, and finds the page where for every letter there is a word, a picture and then a sentence with the word. She then gives Nusrat the book to read from. Meanwhile T1 climbs onto the chair behind Nusrat and becomes quite disruptive. Although Nusrat tries to tell Aisha, not much attention is paid to this little toddler; Aisha continues to instruct Majid with his reading. It is very noticeable throughout that all the children speak in Bangla with Aisha.

Within a short space of time T1 sits next to Nusrat and starts to chant the alphabets and points to the book, this is immediately picked up by Israt who tries to focus T1 onto the reading, Israt says a part and T1 repeats. Meanwhile Majid reads with fervour while Nusrat observes him. From time to time Aisha corrects Majid's reading and spelling, at the same time she prompts Nusrat to read trying to encourage the children to point at the words that they are trying to spell and read as well as to read out aloud.

Regardless of the efforts made by Israt to engage T1 he starts to disrupt the children by crawling on the space behind them and the back of the chairs. All the children start to complain, Aisha then tries to get T1 to come next to her but he refuses by saying that he wants to read from the *siphara* (Chapter 30 of the Qur'an in a booklet form). When all efforts fail Aisha does not remove T1 but re-arranges the children, T1 sits in Nusrat's place and Nusrat sits next to Aisha. At this stage toddler T2 joins the table next to Majid. Once again Aisha manages to engage the three older children in their set tasks of reading. Majid requests Aisha whether he can write and when she agrees he takes out his writing book and gives it to her for her to write in it for him to copy, which she does. Throughout the session the children never hesitated to ask every time they were not sure and Aisha always responded to them with encouragement.

The two toddlers continue to seek Aisha's attention, which they get once all the older children are on task with their writing. She engages by complying with their wishes of wanting to read the Arabic alphabet letters. She searches with T1 until he finds some Arabic alphabet letters which he spots in one of the little pictures and she does the same with T2, where she starts to chant the alphabets and Israt repeats after her while continuing to write. This encourages the toddlers to stay on task.

Aisha ends by reciting a poem from the book and she encourages the children to repeat after her while they continue to write. This activity engages all five children and they are all in tune with each other repeating after Aisha.

(fieldnotes from Ruby, 25/04/06)

These children make up the orchestra and all have a unique role to play within this orchestrated learning, which is being conducted by Aisha.

## How conducting takes place: the intricacies of balance

Aisha's relationship with the children is unlike other caregivers (parents, other grandmothers, siblings, school or complementary school teachers). She has the closeness of a blood grandmother (she is indeed the grandmother of Nusrat and Israt), telling stories and creating a safe space where they can express themselves with ease. She also has the responsibility of a teacher who needs to maintain certain discipline where learning occurs. This means that she is neither a professional like an ordinary school/community class teacher, nor does she have the intimate one-to-one relationship of a blood relative (as she does with Nusrat and Israt). This balance is extraordinarily well maintained by Aisha and is demonstrated by her acceptance of all the children. This is very evident throughout the evening where, alongside the three older children she is teaching, there are two toddlers (T1 and T2) who weave in and out of the teaching zone. Even though the two toddlers are disruptive, Aisha welcomes them into this realm without any reservations and makes them feel a part of the group. It is within this relationship that Aisha has been accepted as a generic grandmother and her relationship with all the children in her class is such that they are all her grandchildren. She is, thus, referred to as *nani* or *nanu* by the children. This is unique to the home setting and unlike any other learning context.

In the excerpt below, Bangla is transliterated. Translations from Bangla are in brackets ( ... ); explanations of the text are in square brackets [ ... ]. In the following transcript the initials M, A and I are used for Majid, Aisha, and Israt. Transcript 1 below is at the beginning of the session where Aisha is trying to teach them the alphabets and transcript 2 takes place towards the end of the session where Aisha is trying to engage T1 into reading from the primer.

## Transcript 1

6M:    (reading out loud from the primer) *shoro-te ozu koro* (shoro is for o-zu) [the Bangla vowel 'shoro' is equivalent to the English sound 'o' and is illustrated through the word o-zu which means to do ablution before prayer]

7A:    *aste aste* (gently gently) [trying to take the book back from M] *shundor kori poro* (read nicely) [she puts it properly in front of him and he carries on reading while she does not do so]

8M:    *shora-te o-zu gosul shikha koro pas wakhto namaz poro* ('shora' is for o-zu, have a bath, learn to pray five times a day)

9A:    *eta shoro shoro-te o-zu* (this is shoro shoro makes o-zu)

## Transcript 2

128A:    *hmm hath dou hath dou* (hmm give your hand give your hand)

129    [T1 starts to point with his left index finger]

130A:    *bam hath na dain hath dou oita tomar dain hath* (not the left hand give your right hand that is your right hand) [pointing to his right hand]

131I:    *nanu Bangla ki bam hath dia lekhle ki guna hoi?* (granny if you write Bangla with your left hand do you commit a sin?)

132A:    *heh bam hath dia shudu, kono kaze bam hath bebohar korte hoi na shudu dan hath* (yes, with the left hand [you should] only ... you should not use your left hand for any work [like writing and eating] just your right hand) [If children are left-handed they are obviously allowed to write using this hand. Aisha is simply pointing out the different uses of each hand]

133　　[she goes back to reading the alphabets again with T2]

Aisha's dual aims for the session are very clear as can be seen in the above transcripts 1 and 2. On the one hand, she wants to teach her group the Bengali vowels using a primer. She uses the sound 'o' (as in orange), which is illustrated through the word 'o-zu', as explained in the transcript. This is the word for ablution, which, as a Muslim, one has to perform before prayer. At the same time this word is a crucial one for her second aim, which is to impart religious and cultural practices. This aim is further illustrated in transcript 2 where she explains the cultural norms of when to use the right and left hands. Aisha's teaching role is, thus, multifaceted. This role contrasts with those of caregivers represented in some studies illustrating theories of scaffolding, guided participation or synergy where these specific teaching objectives are not identified or apparent.

Unlike an ordinary teacher who has to follow an exact curriculum within a set timeframe, Aisha is flexible in that she has multiple ears, ie she listens to all the children working at their own pace, hears when one or two of the children need extra help, and helps them whilst still focusing on another child and helping him/her to read. She encourages observation and listening and attempts to engage even the youngest child, as can be seen in the following extract where even though the toddlers are being disruptive she does not remove them from the table but accommodates them (see lines 128-129 from transcript 2 and lines 10, 33, 34 and 35 from transcript 3), which allows them opportunities to observe and listen. In the following transcript the initials N is used for Nusrat.

## Transcript 3

10　　[A rearranges the seating of the children by letting T1 sit in N's place and moves N next to her]

11A:　*Nusrat hath dia doro* (Nusrat hold with your hand)

12　　[N has a pencil which she uses to point at the words on her page]

13A:　*poro boro kori poro* (read read out aloud) [A strokes N on the back encouragingly]

14N:　*konta portam?* (what shall I read?)

15A:    *shor-o* [first Bangla vowel]

16      [N takes cue and starts to read]

17N:    *Ami sai top line guli phortam* (I want to read the top lines)

18      [A starts to spell the words, she says a part and N repeats after her]

19M:    *nani nani* (granny granny)

20A:    *lekhba ekhon?* (you want to write now?)

21      [M takes out his writing book and gives it to A]

22I:    *ami lekhbo* (I want to write)

23A:    *ekhon na aro poro poro* (not now read more)

24T1:   this mine this mine

25M:    *nani o side-o* (granny on this side)

26      [A starts to turn over pages in M's book]

27M:    *oh etath nai etath nai* (oh it's not here it's not here) [turns to the blank page] *okhan-o okhan-o* (here here)

28A:    *shor-o* [reading out vowel, pointing at N's page and turning to her]

29M:    *okhan-o nani delow lekhia* (write here nani) [the book is facing him] *wrong way wrong way!* [Turns the book around for A]

30      [M then gives A the text book for A to write the part he wants]

31 M:   *ar okhan thaki copy khoro* (and copy from here)

32M:    *ami ockhta sai, ockhta sai ...* (I want this one, this one)

33      [T1 leans over looking at the page]

34T1:   *ami okhta sai ochta sai* (I want this one, this one)

35      [T1, T2 and C look on as A folds the page to make a margin and instructs N while she is doing so]

36A:    *Nusrat tumi banan khoria phoro* (Nusrat you spell and read)

37      [I is reading by herself through spelling each word and asking A every time she is not sure and N is also reading aloud]

The children's relationship with Aisha is both formal in the sense that all the children know they have to achieve targets in terms of their learning, and informal to the extent that they feel comfortable enough to be able to negotiate with her how and what they want to learn. Majid, for example, reads with concentration and enthusiasm so when Aisha feels he needs to move onto a different task she asks him whether he wants to write, as can be seen in transcript 3 (19-21). Majid has full rein of the selection of the text he wants Aisha to write for him to copy, and where he wants to write in the exercise book, but Aisha's flexibility also allows her to meet her objective of the lesson, since by writing from the text of the primer he is able to consolidate what he has just been reading. However, some rigidity is maintained when she turns down the request from Israt (see lines 17-18 below) who wants to write. Aisha does not accept her request as she feels it is not the right time and asks Israt to continue to read:

17I:    *ami lekhbo* (I want to write)

18A:    *ekhon na aro poro poro* (not now read more)

Aisha encourages all the children to read aloud and every so often she herself reads aloud with the children repeating after her. She emphasises the importance of spelling out the words whenever the children attempt to read any of the words in their books. This she does whenever she feels the children are not engaging with the text as well as when they are trying to learn new text. Part of the process of spelling is that the children have to point at what they are trying to spell (see lines 6-8, 36 below):

6A:    *Nusrat hath dia doro* (Nusrat hold with your hand) [A is indicating for N to point to the page and word she is trying to read]

7      [N has a pencil which she uses to point at the words on her page but A wants her to use her finger to point at the words]

8A:    *poro boro kori poro* (read read out aloud) [A strokes N on the back encouragingly]

...

36A:   *Nusrat tumi banan khoria phoro* (Nusrat you spell and read)

Aisha's emphasis on pointing to the text enables the children to focus and also helps her to keep track of what they are saying, as well as providing opportunities for correction and for setting direction. She is thus able to utilise her multiple ears and fulfill her role as a conductor for her very unique orchestra.

## Some concluding thoughts on orchestrated learning

The excerpts outlined above give an idea of why we compare Aisha to the conductor of an orchestra. Like a conductor she must learn the entire score;

in this case for Aisha it is knowing the particular aims she wants each child to address with regard to the linguistic and cultural content of the whole lesson. Aisha demonstrates this, as it is very clear that she has specific aims for this lesson. She wants the children to learn the alphabets as well as acquiring cultural knowledge, specific to the level of each child.

This individualised approach to teaching and leaning is only possible due to the size of the group. Although the children have room to manoeuvre, she makes sure that they each get on with the tasks set at their individual level. Similarly to a conductor of an orchestra who functions as a traffic director for the various sections, Aisha also knows precisely when each child needs to do a different task, just as the instruments enter the musical highway at different times. Aisha demonstrates that she also has to be very diplomatic, since conflicts and disagreements could erupt during the lesson as they do for the conductor during a rehearsal. From the perspective of the children, we see that, like musicians in an orchestra, they may not need to watch the conductor/Aisha directly all the time but just glance at her periodically to insure they are maintaining the proper tempo and dynamics for the piece/lesson. Tempo is the speed at which music/activities are played and it defines the rhythm and pace of a piece of music/lesson.

We believe that orchestrated learning patterns similar to those examined in this chapter may be particularly important to studies on learning in multilingual, cross-cultural contexts, since, whilst probably rare in western interaction, they describe a literacy event that is common in the homes of migrant families. In this chapter, we have focused on the role of the grandmother as conductor or leader of the group. Further studies will be needed to examine the role played by the children as members of this very special orchestra of learners at home.

# Part II:
# Processes of identity formation

# 6

## Constructing cultural and academic identities in community schools: A socio-cultural and dialogical approach

*Evangelia Prokopiou and Tony Cline*

### Introduction

Britain has experienced the growth of diverse immigrant groups, especially Commonwealth immigrants, who came over during the post-war period, and their children comprise the successive generations of British-born young people from ethnic minority backgrounds who are now an important and permanent feature of contemporary British society (Anthias, 2001). Rassool (1999) emphasised the heterogeneity of ethnic minority groups in Britain who, as he argues, 'comprise a rich tapestry of cultural, linguistic and historical experiences grounded in different diasporas that, in turn, have developed within specific socio-historic contexts' (p26).

Community schools, often known as supplementary or complementary schools, have been an important component of the educational experience of many ethnic minority children in Britain. These schools are socio-educational institutions established and run by ethnic minority communities and have a diverse and distinctive pedagogy and aims influenced by the community's needs within specific political and sociocultural contexts.

In this chapter we explore how community schools influence the construction of ethnic minority young people's cultural and academic identities. We seek to understand this by exploring a) what it means to the young people to attend their community school and how they perceive themselves as participants in their school's academic and cultural context and b) what kinds of dialogue young people develop with their cultural communities and its impact on their developing cultural identities. We do so by combining evidence from two contrasting socio-cultural contexts, a Pakistani and a Greek community school. Our claim is that synthesising analyses of findings from different community school settings enables us to develop new approaches to understanding identity processes for ethnic minority pupils who live in multicultural societies.

## The schools and the communities

The Greek school was founded over 20 years ago in a metropolitan area in England and operates in a big mainstream school. Almost 300 children from 4 to 17 years of age attended the school at the time of the research. The teachers come from Cyprus and Greece and there are classes starting from nursery up to and including A-Level classes (Greek literature and language). The school follows the syllabus which has been prepared by the Ministries of Education of Cyprus and Greece designed specifically for Greek children who live abroad. The leaving certificates issued by the school are recognised by the Ministries of Education of Cyprus and Greece. The school runs every Saturday and on a weekday and is partially self-funded through tuition fees but mainly supported, especially in terms of teaching staff, by the Greek and Cypriot Education Missions.

The Pakistani school was founded more than ten years ago and is based at a big mainstream school in a small multi-ethnic south midlands town in England with a student population of over 60 pupils at the time the research took place. The school works with 4 to 18 year old pupils, mainly of Pakistani origin but also from other Muslim backgrounds such as Bangladeshi, Turkish, Somali etc. It offers Arabic, GCSE Urdu, GCSE Islamic Studies and a range of mainstream curricular subjects, mainly English and mathematics as well as preparation for 11+ entrance exams and SATs (annual national assessments in mainstream schools). Additional subjects include arts and crafts, study skills and a variety of PSE topics, all pitched within a culturally relevant context. The school runs every Saturday. A team of ten to twelve teachers and volunteers make up the staff team, supported by an active management and parents' committee. The school has been partially funded through the local authority that supports the work of other ethnic minority voluntary and community based schools and classes in this town.

Identity development needs to be contextualised, that is located within a specific historical and cultural time and space (Hermans, 2003; Valsiner, 2000, 2004). In our study, we have tried to understand each community school by understanding the position of the communities they serve in the context of wider British society. In the following paragraphs, we present a brief overview of the two communities' migration histories with the aim of supporting the interpretation of the analysis later in this chapter.

The mass migration of Pakistanis to Britain started in the late 1950s and early 1960s (Anwar, 1979). The main reasons for their migration were, on the one hand, Britain's need for manual unskilled workers and, on the other hand, immigrants' need to find employment and economic security as well as the colonial links with the host country (*ibid*). The Pakistani community is a heterogeneous one which differs with regards to the areas of Pakistan (eg Punjab, Kashmir) with which Pakistani people most closely identify. Nearly all British Pakistanis are Muslims but they vary in the ways they practice Islam. The Pakistani community is also a diverse community in terms of socio-economical status. In London and the South East, some of the Pakistani communities are well established and their educational achievement is on the same level with, or higher than, national averages. In the West Midlands and the North, the communities have been affected by unemployment, poverty, and social exclusion, and the educational achievement in Pakistani communities is much lower than the national average (RAISE Project). Recent reports (eg Stone and Smith, 2004; Ahmad 2006) describe the impact on British-Muslims of the rise in Islamophobia in Britain after the terrorist attacks in New York on 9/11/2001. As Ahmad (2006) pointed out, 'within minutes of the planes crashing into the twin towers in New York, Islam and terrorism became inseparable, inextricably linked' (p962).

Large-scale Greek-Cypriot migration to Britain started during the last decade of British colonial rule on the island, in the 1950s and 1960s, mainly for economic reasons. However, the Greek-Cypriot community in Britain expanded significantly after the Turkish invasion of the island of Cyprus in 1974. In general, the Greek-Cypriot community is considered to be a well-established and socio-economically successful community with the majority of Greek-Cypriots in business and the professions (Papapavlou and Pavlou, 2001).

## Theoretical background

The theoretical framework of this paper draws on current dynamic psychological approaches to cultural developmental theory (Valsiner, 2000) and the dialogical self theory (Hermans, 2001a) to understand the cultural and dialogical nature of the processes through which ethnic minority youth develop their identities in community schools. These theories present a dynamic view of identities development by paying attention to the interaction between individuals and their sociocultural environments. As Dien (2000) outlined:

> The story of a cultural group is maintained by a tapestry of customs, religion, geography, philosophy, and narratives (myths, legends and historical texts) told in a common language. The shared story provides the individuals with an understanding of cultural norms and values and, most important of all, what constitutes a good person (p5).

The dialogical self theory was greatly influenced by the work of Bakhtin and particularly his interest in the 'multivoicedness of discourse' (Valsiner, 2000). From a dialogical self standpoint, the traditional identity question of 'who am I?' is rephrased as 'who am I in relation to the other?' and 'who is the other in relation to me?' (Hermans, 2003:104). These rephrased questions imply that a person's sense of identity is influenced by his or her relationships with others. Our understanding of this process of influence is increased when the importance of others in one's sense of identity is acknowledged and explored as being part of one's self-system (Hermans, 2003). Ferdman (2000) also argued that the construction of identities needs to be studied in the context of specific historical and cultural realities. In effect, Ferdman defined the task as not only asking 'who am I?' but also 'why am I who I am'? This point is important because it helps to explore the ways minority individuals make sense of themselves: the different ways they come to construct their identities and the different ways their place in a specific socio-historical context influence how they make sense of themselves.

Many authors (eg Hermans and Kempen, 1998; Bhatia and Ram, 2001, 2004) have argued from both a cultural developmental and dialogical perspective that much of the literature on immigrant identity has tended to see ethnic minority young people as being in between two cultures (minority and host). In contrast, the standpoint of cultural and dialogical theories entails a dynamic perspective on the identities of ethnic minority young people. From this standpoint, their identities should not be studied just as static comparisons between various 'beings' (Valsiner, 2004:9), ie being Pakistani or Greek versus being British, but rather as a process through which they are in a constant negotiation of the many aspects that constitute their multiple cultural identities, ie I as a Muslim, I as a Pakistani, I as British etc. As Norton (2000) and others have shown, power relations and social status in society affect multilingual learners' sense of their own identities as well as the opportunities that they have for developing the languages in their repertoire.

## The research method

Episodic interviewing (Flick, 2000) was the main tool for data collection which was used to assess the pupils' experiences and perceptions and understand the underlying dynamics of their community schools and their impact on pupils' developing identities. Individual drawings and group work were used as complementary tools. The participants were sixteen students of Greek/Greek-Cypriot or Pakistani origin with a record of long term attendance at community schools. The students, both girls and boys, were adolescents aged 13 to 18 years, eight in each school. In the Greek school, of the eight participants, two were second generation and two were third generation ethnic minority young persons while for two, one of the parents was born in England and the other in Greece and for the other two, one of the parents was born in England and the other in Cyprus. In the Pakistani school, of the eight participants, for five both parents were born overseas while for three of them one of the parents was born in England and the other overseas.

Interviews in both schools took place both at school premises and at participants' homes. The interviews started by familiarising the interviewee with this specific form of interview, ie 'In this interview, I will ask you to recount situations in your community school' (Flick, 2000) and a clarification of the interview procedure including information regarding the duration of the interview and ethical issues such as confidentiality, anonymity and the right to withdraw. As an interviewer, the main researcher, Evangelia, had an active role and, in many instances, the interviewees were encouraged to comment and correct or confirm the impressions of the interviewer in an attempt to find out as accurately as possible what they meant (Kraus, 2000).

## Situating community schools in context

Interviews with young people from both community schools suggested that the young people had significantly different experiences vis-à-vis the majority community which positioned them in very different worlds. More specifically, the young people in the Greek school thought that Greeks and Greek Cypriots were perceived as having different cultural beliefs and family values from mainstream society but also as being a lively, accepted community with a great historical contribution to Western civilisation. Thalia and Ellie's comments when asked to describe how they thought people in British society perceive Greeks and Greek Cypriots illustrate these perceptions:

> Thalia: ... umm ... I don't think they ... they look at us badly as they would with others because we don't come from an uncivilised background, you know, because we were the ones who invented science and philosophy and everything else

...

> Ellie: I don't know ... think we're loud (laughs) and we are quite cheery people, we are very happy people

In contrast, the young people in the Pakistani school thought that mainstream society perceived Pakistanis as having a different skin colour and religion and as being a community characterised by underachievement, bad behaviour, lack of English language competence, low income and education, cultural barriers and high crime. They reacted with fear and anger to living in post 9/11 British society in which racism and hatred towards Muslims was expressed by identifying Muslims with terrorism. These feelings are echoed in the interview with Fahim:

I:      and, if I'll ask you now how do you feel living in England, in this country?

Fahim:   good ... yeah, okay, good ... probably ... apart from like a bit of racism ... apart from that it's okay.

I:      do you have an example, you know, can you give me a situation where you ... could be personal or not personal ...

Fahim:   well, it's ... like be harder for me to find a job than a white person with the same qualifications ...

I:      are you afraid of that?

Fahim:   not really ... but probably when I get there they might be ... obstacles in the way plus there're ... there're *lot* of anti-Muslim feelings emerging.

I:      and how this makes you feel?

Fahim:   it's always ... sometimes is like ... I don't want to make it obvious, say I'm a Muslim ... well, like terrorism

As seen in the examples above, the dialogue of the participants in the Greek school with their mainstream community was characterised by symmetry, and the young people seemed to have internalised the positive images of their minority group. In contrast, the dialogue of the participants in the Pakistani school with their mainstream society was presented as asymmetrical and power-ridden (Hermans, 2003). The young people in this school described their community as being perceived negatively and in some cases they had internalised the negative views of the majority community. The negative experiences of young people of Pakistani descent in British society may indicate a shift from racial discrimination to religious discrimination which generates new questions regarding the construction and conceptualisation of difference in a post colonial context.

Each community school was perceived by the young people as a place where they could negotiate their relationship with the majority community and gain a solid understanding of their minority cultural identities. The students at the Pakistani school talked as learners of their religion whereas the students at the Greek school talked as learners of the minority culture. Thus, the students of Pakistani origin tended to emphasise the religious values they learned in the school which they saw as guiding their way of life and giving them an understanding of who they were, as the following interview excerpt with Fahim illustrates:

Fahim:   ... umm ... it [the community school] gives me like a ... I'm sort like a sense of identity maybe ...

I:   sense of identity ... how would you define that ... umm ... in which terms, identity?

Fahim:   okay, like a religious and cultural identity ... umm ... probably ... umm ... and also gives me like a place where I can go if I have any questions or stuff like that, I can get some answered ...

I:   what kind of questions?

Fahim:   like ... I don't know ... religious questions something like that ... and importantly it gives me like I learn about my religion and culture.

The participants at the Greek school tended to emphasise the learning of knowledge relevant to their cultural background, values and skills with a stress placed on their use for social purposes, in other words with an emphasis on the social aspects of their cultural engagement.

Ellie: it [the Greek school] makes me like not forget where I'm coming from ... like it makes me remember where I'm coming from and that I'm Greek and just because I'm living in England it doesn't make me English ... I learn Greek and then when I go on holidays to see my family I can talk it more and it's just ... just proves I'm Cypriot

It is perhaps noteworthy that both parents and teachers in the Greek and Greek-Cypriot communities were concerned that the abovementioned values and ways of belonging were under threat because of the assimilation of the next generation of young people within mainstream society.

So the two schools are dynamic socio-educational environments. They influence the development of young people's identities in different ways. Valsiner (2000) argues that formal national education has the effect of distancing young people from their local cultural contexts and reinforces the development of their cultural identities in accordance with values and ways of thinking relevant to the expectations of society at large. In contrast, community schooling appears to develop students' cultural identities in terms of values and ways of thinking in accordance with the expectations of the minority community in which the community school is embedded. Therefore, in the personal and collective journeys of these students' development of identities their community schools act to foster a purposeful cultural closeness between them and their minority communities.

The students of Pakistani origin saw their community school as transmitting shared values and influencing their cultural identity development through the teaching of religion, providing a space to meet other Muslim young people and offering life guidance:

> Azra: ... um ... well, I expect to learn more about my religion, have more experience, meet the people that should be like ... good influence and I should be more focused on my religion and on my duties

In a similar vein, the Greek school was seen as transmitting its cultural values by offering students the opportunity to become part of a community and through this cultural closeness to construct their Greekness:

> Stella: it ... it [the Greek school] sort of gives me an opportunity to mix with Greek people which I probably wouldn't do as much if I didn't come here and I've learned a lot more about my history which I definitely wouldn't have learned and dancing and singing ... I really enjoy like the dancing ...
>
> I: why do you like dancing ... what does it mean to you?
>
> Stella: I don't know ... it's ... the whole Greek culture ... it just makes me feel like ... that I enjoy it ... it's fun ...
>
> I: so when are you dancing how do you feel?
>
> Stella: I feel ... I feel good ... is enjoyable like learning all the Greek ... it makes me feel more Greek (laughs)

For both schools, another way of transmitting cultural values and constructing minority cultural identities was through the teaching of the mother tongue. The students at both schools expressed their appreciation of their mother tongue as a medium of facilitating intrafamily and intracommunity communication and as a cultural tool to understand their cultural backgrounds more fully.

> Bibi: my dad reads Urdu newspapers and it's like so if he's talking about something I can understand or when we went to Pakistan and had some friends with

my mum we spoke Urdu because they did in that part of Pakistan so it was like I can go and understand what they're saying

...

Fahim: Urdu is not just a language, it's like a culture as well ... but also like the way it's talked it gives you a cultural understanding of Pakistan, I think that's important, to like know where you came from and what your culture is

For the students at the Greek school, mother tongue learning was also perceived as a means of preserving their cultural identity, and their general attitude towards it was relevant to their cultural identification.

I:          and, so what does it mean to you to learn Greek?

Thalia:     ... umm ... it's sort of ... helps me know who I am really because if I didn't ... if I couldn't speak Greek, I wouldn't feel as though as a Greek person, I wouldn't feel as a true, you know, Κυπριοπούλα (kipriopoula = Cypriot girl) ... and I think Greek school does help me in being ... speaking Greek helps me sort of get around things and know who I am really

The community school also offered the students the opportunity to develop skills and gain qualifications useful for higher education and work. The difference from a mainstream school context was that this education took place through a strategy of combining academic with cultural knowledge. Students were being educated in subjects that were relevant to their cultural identities.

Zafar: I've been speaking [Urdu] ... I've been speaking as I was ... since I was 2, 3 ... because I used to speak it at home with my mum, my grandparents, my dad ... and ... umm ... now that I've grown older ... umm ... I have more of a need to know my own mother tongue and now it's just come to a GCSE, kind of stage ... and I want to take that subject or as a GCSE ... and if I ... umm ... can study that subject more it'll be a lot easier ... if you learn your mother tongue or learn another language, it's ... it's quite good cause you get extra, kind of skills

...

I: and what do you expect to achieve by coming here?

Orestis: get good GCSE results, be able to speak to my families in Cyprus and Greece and just basically be Greek

## Community schools and socio-cultural guidance

By 'socio-educational guidance' we mean the ways through which the formal or informal curriculum of institutions like community schools entails purposeful promotion of identification with the socio-educational goals and values of these institutions (Valsiner, 2000). As I discussed in the previous section, both community schools held specific expectations of their students, which were in accordance with the socio-educational goals and values of the minority communities in which they were embedded (Valsiner, 2000).

As seen in the models presented in Figures 1 and 2 below, in both community schools a strong academic identity was endorsed to foster the acquisition of knowledge and skills relevant to both their community education and their mainstream and higher education. Although both schools aimed to create a cultural closeness between the students and the minority communities, their goals and methods were different. On the one hand, the Pakistani school aimed to influence the students' cultural identity development mainly through the teaching of religion. The school also aimed to increase self-confidence and strengthen the students' sense of minority identity, how they make sense of themselves as ethnic minority young people, in order to combat negative stereotypes and racism in mainstream society and schools.

In this context, a strong minority identity has an impact not only on the young people's interactions with the minority community but also affects their relationship with mainstream society; the empowerment of their minority identity enables them to relate more confidently to mainstream society (see figure 1). In the Pakistani school, the development of the young people's academic identity was based on the premise that being a good stu-

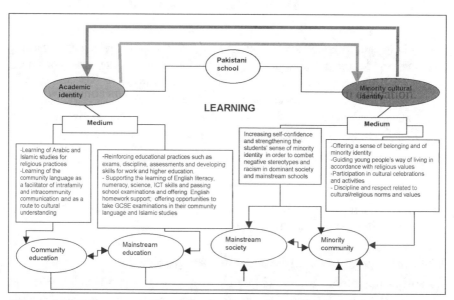

**Figure 1: Development of academic and cultural identities in the Pakistani school**

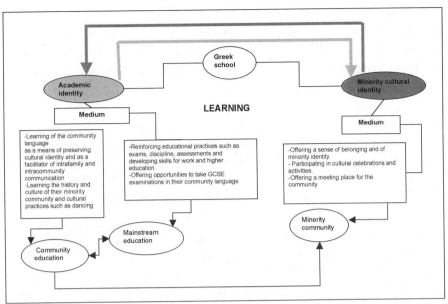

**Figure 2: Development of academic and cultural identities in the Greek school**

dent equalled being a good Muslim. Therefore, the learning of the community language was seen to help students facilitate intrafamily and intra-community communication, gain an understanding of their culture and, equally importantly, to behave in ways that were keeping with Islamic religious principles.

On the other hand, the Greek school aimed to influence the students' minority cultural identity development mainly through sharing similar family and cultural values with other members of the minority community and through the learning of the community language which was perceived as a means of preserving an already threatened minority identity. In this sense, the main aim was the preservation of the community's cultural identity and therefore, and in contrast to the Pakistani school, the focus was mainly on the minority community itself.

In Figure 2 and in contrast to Figure 1 there are no references to mainstream education or mainstream society, because they were not a significant feature of how the Greek school participants described their school during the interviews. In the Greek school, academic identity was based on the premise that being a good student was equated with being a good Greek. Therefore, the learning of the community language was seen as helping students in intra-family and intra-community communication and preserving the minority cultural identity. In addition, academic identity was linked with earning an extra GSCE and helped students develop skills useful for mainstream education. In this way, academic identity within community schools was developing in a parallel process with cultural identity, both present in a dialogical relationship.

## The development of multiple identities in a diverse society

These schools are located in a multicultural society where young people are developing multiple identities. The students in both community schools talked about aspects of differences and similarities and belonging within their majority and minority communities as well as living in a multicultural society. This negotiation resulted in multiple identities which emerged through a constant positioning and re-positioning within their communities and wider society. The flexibility to incorporate all of these various positions was described as a defining characteristic of their multiple identities and as something which broadened their horizons and opportunities rather than an ambivalence or lack of clarity in relation to who they were. In other words, their identity as a process of intra-construction, that is, the process of constructing our multiple identities within ourselves, was characterised by dialogical oppositions rather than by conflicts or tensions, as seen in the following two extracts, one from each school:

Jehan: I'd say [pause] I'm a Pakistani ... um ... but I'm not as ... I have a culture that side but ... um ... I'm more in between kind of ... I'm not rejecting my culture ... kind of extending it kind of ... which is a western culture and ...

I: extending it to the western ...

Jehan: yeah ... but at the end I am Jehan (laughs)

I: and in which ways do you feel different, if you feel different ... .?

Lydia: umm ... I don't really ... I don't feel different.

I: and, in general, you know, to be of Greek Cypriot background in England, how do you experience that?

Lydia: ... umm ... it's nice because there is no like ... separate British culture ... it's nice to have another culture and then being British

However, from a dialogical standpoint it is essential to acknowledge the importance of others in one's sense of identity. From that theoretical viewpoint in which identity is seen as a process of inter-construction, that is the process of constructing our multiple identities through our interaction with others, the negotiations of the participants from the Pakistani school were characterised by more conflicts.

Earlier in this chapter I discussed the young people's reaction to being negatively stereotyped by the majority community. It could be argued that the dialogue between their intra-construction and inter-construction processes must be seen as having been blocked because the opposites were not dialogically related. For example, Fahim said that being negatively stereotyped as a Muslim made him to want to be invisible as a Muslim. Such a dialogue reduces the multivoiced character of young people's multiple identities and moves them towards a monological direction (Hermans, 2003). For the participants in the Pakistani school, being discriminated against by the majority society generated fears for the future and subordinated the minority aspect of their cultural identity. The Pakistani community school could make a major contribution in fostering the multivoiced nature of the young people's developing cultural identities.

## Conclusion

The aim of this chapter was to demonstrate the analytical insights of examining community schools within contrasting communities. It has shown that when thinking of community schools, we need to contextualise them within their communities and take into consideration each community's trajectory in relation to both its origins and the mainstream society. By acknowledging the different developmental paths taken by different minority communities in mainstream society, this chapter strongly suggests that community schools in Britain are developing differently and in accordance with the needs and goals of each minority community.

Moreover, it aimed at contributing to the development of theorising how cultural and academic identities are fostered in community schools. Etymologically, identity means 'the same' (derived from the Latin root *idem*). The findings of this study showed that far from staying the same, these young persons' cultural and academic identities are constantly constructed and reconstructed through dialogical relationships within themselves and others. These dialogical relationships are influenced by historical, economic and political discourses which are constructed both within and beyond their cultural and educational worlds. Community schools can play a crucial role in helping ethnic minority young people's negotiation of their multiple identities across various sociocultural contexts. Future research in community education needs to explore the distinctive features of the ethos of each community school and trace the roots of that ethos in the position of the community in the wider society.

# 7

# Chinese complementary school pupils' social and educational subjectivities

*Becky Francis, Louise Archer and Ada Mau*

## Introduction

C hinese complementary schooling is particularly long-established in the UK. The majority focus principally on teaching in Cantonese rather than Putonghua, reflecting the heritage of the largest proportion of those of Chinese heritage living in Britain as the majority of Chinese migrants to Britain arrived from Hong Kong, particularly from the New Territories region, in the 1950s and 1960s. We are currently experiencing a new wave of migration to Britain from Mainland China. However, many of these migrants remain 'outside the system', and have not in any case been in Britain long enough to establish families with school-age children.

The number of Putonghua schools is, however, increasing and the powerful discourse of Chinese economic success has provoked a surge of enthusiasm for Putonghua, leading many traditionally Cantonese schools to offer additional lessons in Putonghua. Given their focus on language, it might be assumed that the sole purpose of these institutions is to perpetuate the Chinese spoken and written language in younger generations. However, a diverse international literature asserts a range of other benefits and intentions of Chinese complementary schooling. These include, for example, the provision of educational capital in relation to mainstream schooling (Zhou and Li, 2003; Zhou and Kim, 2006), multilingual creativity (Li Wei, 2006), a shared community space to facilitate intra-ethnic interaction, (Zhou and Kim, 2006; Creese *et al*, 2008) and replication of culture (Wang, 1996; Chow, 2004).

Although the various benefits of complementary schooling are well documented, including in this book, research on the perceptions and experiences of complementary schools among the user populations, especially the pupils, has been scant. Our research sought to make a distinctive contribution by focusing on how British-Chinese pupils and their parents construct complementary schooling, and on the impact of complementary schooling on pupils' social and learning identities.

We adopt a broadly poststructuralist approach to notions of culture and identity, drawing on Foucault's work on discursive power (eg 1972, 1980), and on Chun's poststructuralist interrogation of the notion of Chinese culture (1996), to recognise how identities, and concepts such as culture, are discursively produced. These discourses on the constitution of Chineseness and Chinese culture delineate truth, fixity and status and are infused with desire and morality. In contrast to positions that produce culture as a fixed, static and definable entity, our theoretical approach recognises that the construction of boundaries around culture, eg what counts and should be taught/preserved, is a social and political process (Hall, 1990; Chun, 1996; Creese *et al*, 2006). We have argued elsewhere that complementary schooling itself provides an example of such practices, because what commentary on this topic often overlooks is the highly politicised and stratified nature of language, and its power as a system of reification and/or marginalisation (Francis *et al*, 2009).

Complementary schools tend to teach a particular language at least primarily, presenting a unity where actually there may have been diversity, and often albeit unintentionally reifying one language at the expense of others (see also Chapters 2 and 3). This has certainly been the case in Chinese complementary schools, which have tended to focus exclusively on Cantonese as the language of status in Hong Kong, at the expense of other languages spoken by the Hong Kong population (Francis *et al*, 2009). The point is further illustrated by the rapid increase in Putonghua lessons within these schools since Hong Kong's reversion to China in 1997, and Mainland China's rise as a global economic power. Such promotion of particular languages over others for instrumental reasons raises issues of language and identity, which will be further drawn out in this chapter.

We use this chapter to articulate some of the key findings from our study. In the first part we discuss the apparent impact of complementary schooling on our British-Chinese respondents' subjectivities, focusing on their social and education identities. In the second part we examine more closely pupils' productions of the benefits of their Chinese schooling, in relation to issues of subjecthood and identity.

## Methods

The research, funded by the Economic and Social Research Council (RES-000-23-1513), was conducted across six different Chinese schools. Three are located in London where a third of the total Chinese population in Britain reside (Census, 2001); the others in different English metropolitan areas: Manchester, Liverpool and Birmingham. The sample includes only schools primarily teaching Cantonese although Putonghua is in some cases taught as a secondary language, as these represent the established British-Chinese community rather than new migrants (Parker, 2000).

As many Chinese school classes are based on ability rather than age, we took a decision to focus the research on 11-13 year old pupils rather than discrete classes, but including older pupils too where necessary. Research methods included ethnographic observation and documentary analysis, and interviews with teachers and parents. The data considered in this chapter is drawn from interviews with 60 pupils. The 60 pupils included 36 girls and 24 boys, of whom 52 (87%) were British-born Chinese. Of the remaining eight pupils, four were born in Mainland China, two in Hong Kong, one elsewhere, and one pupil was mixed heritage (Chinese/White). Twenty-five (42%) of these respondents were from working-class backgrounds, with an additional seventeen (28%) from families with small businesses. Twenty-seven per cent were from middle-class families, with a further three per cent (2 pupils) un-assigned.

We recognise that categorising British-Chinese respondents according to social class is particularly challenging: many authors have documented how and why recent Chinese diasporic trajectories have in Britain been directed through the catering trade, and we discuss elsewhere how British conceptions of social class as delineated by the Registrar General Scale are inadequate to address the complexity of the British-Chinese case (Archer and Francis, 2007). For pragmatic purposes we have distinguished between clearly working class respondents (including, for example, restaurant waiters, and those working for others in take-aways), and small business owners (owners of take-aways and small restaurants) – the latter of whom might be automatically categorised as middle-class in British social class categorisations, yet actually may have few (if any) educational qualifications and may be working all hours in a family business to ensure it survives (for further detail of our methods of categorisation, see Archer and Francis, 2007).

## British-Chinese pupils' experiences of complementary schooling in relation to their productions of subjectivity

Our mapping revealed that the population of Cantonese Chinese Schools is overwhelmingly comprised of second generation rather than third generation pupils. In our sample, 97 per cent of children had at least one parent born overseas, and 88 per cent reported speaking Chinese at home with 63 per cent of pupils speaking only Cantonese at home. In addition, a high proportion have parents who work in the catering trade, rather than representing those second generation parents who have moved to less ethnicised, middle-class/ professional areas of work. This finding raises important issues, as we shall elaborate in the discussion section. Particularly, it raises questions as to the absence of the rapidly-growing third generation of British-Chinese, particularly dual heritage young people (Song, 2009).

We found that many teachers and parents and a few pupils in our sample constructed Chinese complementary schools as explicit cultural projects, producing Chinese culture as definable, and its reproduction as necessarily beneficial. However, such expectations appeared from our analysis to precipitate a range of tensions both conceptual and in practice. For instance, where schools authorise particular hegemonic notions of Chineseness, these tend to involve an ossification of culture that is conceptually problematic, politically charged representing a Cultural China discourse (see Ang, 1998) and potentially off-putting to pupils being viewed by many young people as outmoded (see Archer *et al* forthcoming, also Chapter 3). Our findings show that whilst schools tend to have the explicit aim of preserving culture and encouraging pupils to feel more Chinese, their success in this respect is complicated. Pupils were divided as to whether attendance made them feel more (or less) Chinese. Thirty-one pupils (52%) agreed that it did make them feel more Chinese. For example, Joanne Tse (Yew Chung) explains 'the more you go to Chinese school, the more Chinese you feel. I don't know, I feel more Chinese anyway coming here'.

However, half the pupils rejected such readings of impact of complementary schooling on Chinese identity, 28 (47%) pupils disagreed, and one was undecided. Those who felt that the schools did bolster a sense of Chineseness declared this was not on the basis of the school's formal cultural agenda, but due to learning the language and through the mere fact of being with other British-Chinese. Joanne Tse went on to describe the novelty of being surrounded by Chinese people at her Chinese school and of not, for once, being the only Chinese pupil in class as she was in her mainstream school. So Chinese schools provided a valued space in which the imagined community could be tangibly experienced, hence facilitating discourses of community and belonging. Our findings here, then, support previous work on the comforting and sustaining features of ethnic enclaves, and their offer of momentary respite from minoritisation (Creese *et al*, 2006). This provision of a critical mass may be especially important for Chinese groups due to their distinctive geographical dispersal in the UK resulting in their frequently comprising a minority of minorities within mainstream schooling.

This community aspect of complementary schooling in turn facilitated the other key aspect we found to contribute to pupils' Chinese or BBC (British-born Chinese) identities: provision of opportunity for young people to engage in contemporary youthful cultural forms with their peers. The young people's constructions of ethnic identity were far more likely to draw on contemporary, diasporic, youth cultural formations than the more traditional perceptions of parents and teachers. So, ironically, the pupils' constructions of Chineseness were often set against dominant school versions and may be indicative of the young people's attempts to find ways to rework their own notions of cultural authenticity. When asked about their ethnic self-identification, young people constructed a range of ethnic identities (eg as Chinese, British-Chinese, British-born Chinese and British), which evoked more complex notions of identity and Chineseness than their elders (see also Chapter 6). Max Fong's (Rossmoor) reflection on his identification is illustrative of such hybridity: 'Not British-born Chinese, I wouldn't say [that]. But I'd say like half English, half sort of Chinese. I was born half Chinese and half English. I don't really go onto one side – I don't really say Chinese most of the time, but I say English and Chinese'.

However, it is notable that very few young people in our sample identified as simply British or English, or did not mention their Chineseness. Given the nature of the sample, and the context of the interviews (in complementary schools), it is possible that this reflects the impact of their complementary schooling on their subjectivities. Further research with young British-Chinese not attending Chinese school would be needed to test this hypothesis.

The study also explored pupils' constructions of their experiences within Chinese schools in relation to their learning and learner identities. Pupils tended to feel that they learn best in mainstream schooling. However, this was predominantly explained as due to the shorter duration of complementary schooling. Pupils also identified a range of practices within Chinese schools that they felt supported their learning and fitted with their learner identities. These included: the competition and reward culture which they relished, greater teacher involvement, closer relations between teachers and pupils than those they experienced in mainstream schooling and small teaching group sizes. These perceptions were not dependent on social class or gender. Pupils especially appreciated the holistic pedagogic approach adopted by many teachers. These positive responses constitute an important finding, given criticisms in the wider literature about the quality of teaching in complementary schools (Li Wei, 2006).

Many students felt that they were able to celebrate their love of learning in a way not possible in mainstream schooling, and that they could do so among like-minded peers. Moreover, our analysis reveals a construction of Chinese schooling among pupils that appeared to facilitate adoption of more playful learner identities in Chinese school, in relation to their reported more diligent attitudes to mainstream schooling (cf. Li Wei and Wu, 2009, also Chapter 3). Young people reported feeling more comfortable and relaxed in Chinese schools, and felt able to be 'noisier' and sometimes 'cheekier' than in mainstream schools. Such behaviours were indeed recorded in our classroom observations. Hence it appears from our analysis here, in relation to our previous work examining British-Chinese pupils' experiences of mainstream schools (Archer and Francis, 2007), that pupils may produce different subjectivities in the complementary schooling environment, perhaps in relation to different interpellations and expectations by teachers and other spectators. Pupils' more playful and even resistant subjectivities within complementary school were facilitated by factors such as the absence of experience of racism, no formal punishment systems and less pressure to achieve. The Chinese language qualification was rarely linked to A Level or university entrance requirements.

## Pupils' constructions of the purposes and benefits of complementary schools

The overwhelming majority of pupil respondents saw the purpose of their complementary schools and their attendance of them as perpetuating proficiency in the Chinese language. Forty-eight pupils (80%) said that they attend Chinese school to learn/improve their Chinese, with only a few volunteering other reasons. This was the case irrespective of respondents' social class or gender. This construction of Chinese schools as heritage language institutions contrasts with findings elsewhere – the United States, for example – that Chinese schools are seen as supplementary to mainstream education, intending to improve the social and educational capital of users. As Zhou and Li (2003) and Zhou and Kim (2006) have elaborated, Chinese schools in the

United States include an often explicit focus on improving mainstream educational performance in various subjects, as well as providing information and preparation for successful college entrance.

Some young people in our study did see learning Cantonese as instrumentally beneficial, as a practical skill with which to increase their marketability in the global workplace. These pupils frequently mentioned a benefit of attendance of complementary schools as the gaining of exam credentials (GCSE, and sometimes A level), and/or as an additional skill to list on one's CV. For example, Matt Huang (Yew Chung) explains, 'it's like expanding your skills: you can learn French, English and Chinese and at the moment I'm learning Japanese as well, but that's in English school; so it's just expanding your skills'. And Michelle Lee (Monterey) surmises of Chinese, 'It will definitely be another skill on your CV, so when you go for a job interview they will look at your CV and say 'Oh you know more than one language' so that will definitely be a positive point'.

We maintain that this constitutes an interesting example of pupils refusing the tendency within Western discourse for their mother-tongue education to be positioned as irrelevant, and rather re-investing this language skill as an 'ethnic capital' to benefit their saleability in the global labour market. Pupils such as those quoted here saw Chinese as an additional credential for their CVs to facilitate opportunities and careers wherever they were based, not limited to China, Hong Kong or the UK.

We use the term ethnic capital tentatively, as an important but possibly controversial concept. It may be that the relative global power of heritage nation and popular images of such nations in the West, impact and either facilitate or constrain the mobilisation of such capital. For example, China is a rapidly increasing global economic power, and hence Chinese language skills may be more likely to be viewed positively. Nevertheless, we feel that the concept of mother-tongue language as ethnic capital encapsulates a valid distinction between the mobilisation of a minoritised community language as in the case of Cantonese Chinese in Britain, and the mobilisation of foreign languages as capital more generally, for example, the case of white pupils learning Putonghua in public or mainstream school. As we might expect, social class appeared salient here. Among the small number of pupils articulating this position, none were working class, raising the likelihood that their social class positioning provides the social capital necessary to facilitate the re-working of community language as ethnic capital. In other words, that the middle-class British-Chinese pupils' cultural capital facilitates the envisioning or re-cognition of community language as a marketable skill.

We have already observed how the population of Chinese schools may not accurately reflect the British-Chinese population in the UK. For those mainly second-generation pupils attending Chinese school, however, we found the schools to play an important role in supporting diasporic existence in the UK. These pupils tended to retain strong links to Hong Kong. Most had extended family in Hong Kong and annual trips back to Hong Kong were common among our sample. Hence, application of the language skills they learnt in complementary schools when in Hong Kong, and in accessing facets of Hong Kong popular culture, eg Cantopop, Chinese soap operas, constituted a strong incentive for pupils' learning. Jessica Lee (Kentfield) relays how she and her sister enjoy 'all these Taiwanese dramas and Japanese dramas, that's fashionable in Hong Kong', expanding, 'yeah on the internet you can watch dramas and stuff, like TVB dramas, and download Hong Kong music, music videos on YouTube and stuff like that.'

For many, learning Chinese was also necessary for facilitating communica-tion with relatives in the UK. As Albert Leung (Kentfield, aged 13) explains, if he could not speak Chinese 'I wouldn't be able to communicate with my Mum because ... they don't know some English, they only know how to speak some of it.' Time and again, pupils described how parents and grandparents, particularly mothers and grandmothers, have little or no English, and hence the fundamental necessity of competence in Chinese for inter-generational communication. For other pupils, learning to read and write in Chinese pro-vided a skill that could help family members who were not literate in Chinese.

What emerges here is the practical application of the Chinese that pupils develop in complementary schools, in communication and translation back and forth between different languages and vehicles of communication, eg English to Chinese, Chinese writing to Chinese speech, and so on. These practices are produced as the integral, unremarkable mechanisms of com-munication and survival within diasporic habitus. Mother-tongue language facilitates, but also gives access to, these networks and links. In this sense, complementary schools may be seen as pivotal institutions for facilitating the continued interface with the heritage country and its popular culture, and communication between generations.

Pupils often saw proficiency in Chinese as the key signifier of Chinese identity. Time and again, pupils responded that they needed to learn the Chinese language because they are Chinese: Wai Yan Lee (Monterey) explains it is important he learn Chinese 'because Chinese people learn Chinese'; and Lihuan Yang (Monterey) agrees, 'Because it's what I am, is like Chinese'. For these pupils, it seemed to be unquestioned that as Chinese people they ought to be able to speak Chinese. Many seemed puzzled at our question, reflecting the taken-for-granted position they appeared to adopt in relation to the answer. Indeed, the perceived necessity for young people of Chinese origin to be proficient in the Chinese language emerged as grounded in powerful moral discourses of duty, identity and inclusion/exclusion, which appeared to retain a profound hold on the experiences and understanding of identity among pupils across social class groups. This is illustrated in the following responses:

I:    OK. How come you wanted to come here then? Why are you interested?

R:    Well it's because I'm Chinese so I should actually learn Chinese.

I:    So do you think it matters if *you* couldn't speak Chinese then?

R:    Yeah. It would be a disgrace if I couldn't speak Chinese, yeah!
      (Pui Ming Cheung [Avery])

I:    So why is it important for you to learn the Chinese language?

R:    Because I'm Chinese. A Chinese person doesn't know Chinese is an extreme disgrace.
      (Yong Jie Zhang [Pui Kui])

There were many more such responses in our data, and it is important to note the highly-charged language pupils used – words such as 'disgrace', 'embarrassing', 'shun' – emotive words evoking powerful tropes of shame/pride, exclusion/inclusion. Indeed, many of the pupils who used such language initially seemed to struggle to articulate their responses when prompted about them (Francis *et al*, 2008). However, not all the pupils were so reticent. Oreina Yip (Avery) explains:

I:    And do you think it's important for you to learn the Chinese language?

R:    Yeah as a Chinese person I think it is really important

I:    Why do you say that?

R:    Because like I said before, if you're Chinese and you only speak something like English it's still a little embarrassing. If a Chinese person comes up to you and starts speaking Chinese and you don't understand it's really embarrassing. Like they say in Chinese, the BBCs who don't speak Chinese are like bananas because they're Chinese on the outside and inside they're completely English.

The application here of the concept of the banana is particularly interesting in theoretical terms, because of the apparent slight distinction from the more widely-known concept of the coconut (black on the outside, white on the inside) which it echoes. Both metaphors suggest that racial embodiment is insufficient in itself to constitute one as authentically black or yellow: one's identity, as well as one's body, must delineate the appropriate ethnicity in order for one to be considered authentic. Yet there appears a subtle difference between the two cases in what may be considered as constituting identity. For these Chinese pupils the Chinese language appears to be a key or perhaps the delineator of Chinese identity. In the Chinese case as it is presented by our respondents, language appears to subsume and express identity, rather than the other way around.

Our analysis of the emergent view of language as culture/identity raises important questions around the conception of ethnic identity. The young people's discussion of the importance of knowing Chinese, and what they saw as the implications of failure (disgrace, embarrassment, exclusion) raises different issues. The moral and penalising discourses of pride/shame, duty/rejection, inclusion/exclusion, proficiency/deficiency underpinning their statements clearly exercised a discursive power evident in the emotional response produced, and may be argued to constitute a strong pressure on children of Chinese heritage to conform to this reproduction. It may be that these discursive mobilisations are produced to counter the dominant discourses circulating in Western society which position Western epistemologies and practices as normative and superior, and Other practices as abject and invalid (Ang, 1998) and the consequent inducement to abandon those values and language practices deemed as constituting Chinese culture within a Western society. So in other words, moral pressure for Chinese language competence among British-Chinese youth from British-Chinese adults that appears to reflect nationalist/conservative sentiments may be driven by defensiveness due to British-Chinese minoritisation in British society. Anthias and Yuval-Davis (1992) have discussed how such anxieties and experiences of threat among minority ethnic groups may be expressed in a tightening of boundaries regarding what is seen to constitute authentic identity and culture.

## Concluding discussion

We hope to have illustrated some of the ways in which British-Chinese pupils construct their identities within a complementary school context, and the impact of complementary schooling on their subjectivities. We have explained how the over-whelming majority of British-Chinese pupils attending

complementary schools see the purpose of these schools and their attendance of them as perpetuating proficiency in the Chinese language and how
many of these pupils produce a notion of ethnic identity as constituted by
language (see also Chapter 1). Pupils often saw proficiency in Chinese as the
key signifier of Chinese identity. This production of language as culture/
identity raises theoretical questions about the conception of ethnic identity,
and about constructed binaries concerning heritage language competency
that position young people as adequate or inadequate; Chinese or not properly Chinese.

It may be argued that this understanding of the purpose of complementary
school as being to perpetuate heritage language may reflect the demographics of those attending Cantonese complementary schools. As we have
seen, attendees represented diverse social class groups, but professional
families constituted a small minority of the attendees in our sample (12%).
Moreover, the vast majority of pupils in our sample were second generation,
with at least one parent born overseas (97%), and often speaking Chinese to
some extent at home (88%).

We have shown how this gave the young people in our study very close links
to Hong Kong in particular. Yet such experiences may be decreasingly repre-
sentative of the British-Chinese community as a whole. Even if we focus exclusively on those of Hong Kong heritage rather than the arrivals from Mainland China, third generation young people remain significantly under-repre-
sented in our study. This begs the question as to why they appear not to be
attending Chinese school: is it that they no longer see the mother-tongue as
important? Or perhaps that the teaching methods and expected oral proficiency practiced at Chinese schools are excluding to them, as our ethnographic data shows that teachers overwhelmingly speak in Chinese within
lessons (see Mau *et al*, 2009)? These questions comprise important areas of
further research. Our analyses emphasise how, like mainstream schooling,
Chinese schooling cannot be isolated from the social, political, historic and
economic factors that impact on schools and their users, and position them
in particular ways.

For those attending Chinese school, we have seen how these schools play an
important role in supporting the diasporic existence of the Chinese in the UK
and providing spaces within which young people may construct and experience British-Chinese subjectivities. Indeed, they may be read as pivotal
institutions for facilitating the continued interface with the heritage nation
and its popular culture, and communication between generations. Further,

we have highlighted how the ethnic enclave of the Chinese school offers sanctuary from the pervasive minoritisation and exoticisation that the pupils experience in wider society (Creese *et al*, 2006).

Yet whilst schools tend to have the explicit aim of preserving culture and encouraging pupils to feel more Chinese, we have shown that their success in this respect is complicated. Pupils who do feel more Chinese as a result of their attendance reported doing so not on the basis of the school's cultural agenda, but through the mere fact of being with other Chinese, which provided a valued space in which the community could be tangibly experienced. We suggested that this may be especially important for Chinese young people due to their distinctive geographical dispersal in the UK.

The other main factor in the schools' success in promoting Chineseness was identified as providing young people with the opportunity to engage in contemporary youthful cultural forms with their peers. Ironically, these constructions of Chineseness were set against dominant school versions and, we suggest, are indicative of the young people's attempts to find ways to rework their own notions of cultural authenticity. In this respect, we suggest that schools could usefully reconsider the value of an ossified cultural agenda within the contemporary diasporic space. For example, schools could open spaces for multilingualism and for experimentation with contemporary, hybridised social identities.

We suggest that such schools can be understood as complex sites in the production and contestation of diasporic cultural identities. They are not innocent projects, as any attempts to define the boundaries of culture and identity are inherently and inevitably political acts. Yet these schools are often highly valued by pupils, parents and teachers and can be understood as performing a range of valuable and important functions. However, we do feel that there may be scope for a more useful, critical and nuanced engagement with issues of culture and re-workings of what might be included within notions of British-Chinese identity within these spaces, particularly if, as Ang argues, we are 'to seize on the radical theoretical promise of the diasporic perspective' (2001:241).

Note: Some material in this chapter was originally covered in the article 'Language as Capital, or Language as Identity? Chinese complementary school pupils' perspectives on the purposes and benefits of complementary schools' (B. Francis, L. Archer and A.Mau), published in *British Educational Research Journal*, vol 35 (4); the authors would like to thank Routledge for permission to use it here.

# 8

# Language choice and identity negotiations in a Brazilian Portuguese community school

*Ana Souza*

## Introduction

This chapter tells the story of three mixed-heritage children, a girl, Josefa, and two boys, Benedito and Antônio. Taking a social constructionist view of identity (Rao, 1999), it explores the multiple ways they draw on different sets of linguistic resources (Portuguese and English) to negotiate aspects of their learner identities in a Brazilian Portuguese community language school. The data discussed here are part of a larger study which focused on language and identity issues from the perspective of a group of Brazilian mothers married to men of another nationality, and their mixed-heritage children (Souza, 2006). The children's views on their identities were explored through interviews and their actual identity negotiations were investigated through observations and audio recordings of teacher-pupil exchanges and informal peer talk during the lesson.

## Identity and language choice

Creese *et al* (2006) explore the links between language and identity among children of Gujarati heritage in complementary schools in Leicester, UK. They identify three identity positionings available to the children: heritage, multi-cultural and learner identities. The first two identities are associated with ethnic group belonging, whereas the third refers to how the complementary school contributes to the development of a successful learner identity across learning contexts. The children in my study also show that they value their learner identities. However, the learner identities they develop in the context of the Brazilian Portuguese community schools seem to differ in important ways from those developed by the aforementioned Gujarati heritage children. In the case of the Gujarati heritage children, their learner identities were closely connected to obtaining mainstream qualifications and being successful in the mainstream school. Such a focus seems to be absent in the Brazilian Portuguese school in this study. This may be because the children studied were aged 5 to 12 years and therefore too young to sit for mainstream examinations. In addition, the school had no links with the mainstream educational system and the teachers did not try to make any connections between learning Portuguese and the instrumental value of becoming bilingual and biliterate more generally. Instead, the teachers and parents involved in the school focused on promoting connections between the children's heritage language and their ethnic (Brazilian Portuguese) identities.

Mills (2001) focuses on the importance of language in the maintenance of a group of children's sense of identity as being both British and Pakistani. These children, like the ones in this study, emphasise the importance of their linguistic repertoire in linking it to their heritage, family and community. In this sense, they experience multiple identities. The concept of multiple identities is based on the assumption that identities are not fixed but socially constructed (Rao, 1999). A Brazilian in London, for instance, may have any of the following identity options at his/her disposal: South American, Brazilian, Catholic, mixed-heritage, middle-class, female, wife, mother, language learner, professional, amongst others. One could see identity as a big box full of cards representing many different options. Some may be negotiable, others contested and others may be found to be non-negotiable. Although the cards are interconnected, only the relevant ones are taken out of the box according to context and participants.

## The community and the school

England has become one of the countries in Europe with a high concentration of Brazilian immigrants. The estimated number of Brazilians in the UK is about 200,000 (Evans *et al,* 2007). The community makes itself present in England through cultural events which include artists who come from Brazil to perform as well as from groups who have settled in England and elsewhere. It is possible to attend religious services held by the Catholic and Protestant churches as well as other religions which have mainly developed in Brazil, such as Kardecism and Afro-Brazilian cults. Moreover, services ranging from tarot reading to legal services can be accessed in Portuguese. The Brazilian community has also shown interest in maintaining Portuguese language and culture through children's groups organised by Brazilian mothers. The number of groups changes constantly but according to the Brazilian Association of Educational Projects in the UK, four are active in London at time of writing, one of which offers literacy classes in Portuguese. It is this which is the focus of my chapter.

The Brazilian Portuguese school in this study is the only one which focuses on developing the children's oral as well as literacy skills in Portuguese. The school was founded by a group of mothers and was organised according to three different levels at the time of the data collection: level 1 for children aged 5-8 whose purpose was to develop the children's oral skills; level 2 for children aged 5-8 who had already acquired oral competence and were developing their literacy skills; and level 3 for children aged 8-12 who wanted to develop their literacy skills even further. The lessons at the school took place on Saturdays and were two hours long with a break for a snack. There were about ten children in each level.

## Three mixed-heritage children

In this chapter, I focus on three children, Josefa, Benedito and Antônio, who attended the Brazilian Portuguese school over many years. Josefa and Benedito were in level 2 while Antônio was in level 3. In both levels, the teachers worked with the children to develop their listening, speaking, reading and writing skills but used a different curriculum and teaching materials reflecting their age and competence in Portuguese.

Josefa was enrolled in the school at the age of 4 and was 8 years old at the time of the field work. Her mother reported speaking to her only in Portuguese and taking her to Brazil once a year. The sustained home and school input in Portuguese had enabled Josefa to be competent in Portuguese. She reported enjoying travelling to Brazil as well as being part of the Brazilian community in London, interacting in Portuguese and attending the Brazilian school. Although Josefa appeared to consider Brazil her place of birth and Portuguese as definer of her identity, she also acknowledged the influence of English and British culture in her life.

Although born and raised in England, Benedito was used to being addressed in Portuguese by his mother as well as many other Brazilians with whom his family had shared accommodation over the years. This experience had equipped Benedito with a good passive command of Portuguese. However, his active competence was almost none before starting the school at the age of 6. The school input has enabled Benedito to be actively competent in

Portuguese and he is now fluent in both Portuguese and English, as revealed in the classroom recordings when he was 8. Benedito self-identifies as English because he was born in England.

Although born and raised in London, Antônio lived in Brazil, where he attended nursery. He understands, speaks, reads and writes in both Portuguese and English. Antônio started attending the Brazilian school when it first opened at the age of 7 and was 11 at the time of the classroom recordings. Antônio self-identifies as being both English and Brazilian and identifies his parents' place of birth and their background as salient features of his ethnic identity. Nonetheless, Antônio seems to have more cultural links to the Brazilian culture than to the Portuguese language. It appears that English is not only his preferred language but also the one he uses more often.

## The children's language choice and identity negotiations

Below I discuss aspects of the children's language choices and identity negotiations as they interact with their teachers and peers in the Brazilian Portuguese school and probe into the motivations for their choices.

When at school, I observed that Josefa only speaks Portuguese, perhaps reflecting her reported pride in her linguistic skill. As in other chapters in this book (eg Chapters 1-4) much of the lessons in school are teacher-centred and teacher-controlled, which does not allow for many pupil-initiated interactions. In the following example, we see this teacher-controlled interaction as Josefa (J) is called upon by the teacher (T) to explain a whole class activity to a newcomer.

### Example 1

    1T: *Quem gosta de pipoca?*
        [Who likes popcorn?]
        (Josefa is not answering any of the questions, which are asked to the whole group. The teacher then shows on the board that Josefa's name and the new student's name, although pronounced in the same way, are spelled differently. The teacher then addresses Josefa directly.)

    2T: *A Josefa t'aqui?*
        [Is Josefa here?]

    3J: *Sim.*
        [Yes.]

    4T: *Qual o nome dela?*
        [What's her name?]

5J: *Ana.*

6T: *Josefa, explica pra Ana como é o Adivinha O Que É*
[Josefa, explain the riddles activity to Ana.]

7J: *Ela tem que falar um monte de coisa e você tem que adivinhar o que é.*
[She (the teacher) has to say a lot of things and you have to guess what it is.]

8R: *Como é que eu adivinho?*
[How do I guess?]

9T: *XXXX tem que falar o nome de coisa.*
[XXXX (the teacher) has to say the name of the thing.]

10T: *O que é o que é?*
[What is ... ?]

The teacher addresses the students informally *Quem gosta de pipoca?* [Who likes popcorn?] (line 1) illustrating that Portuguese is the default language of classroom interaction. Josefa only starts to participate from line 2 onwards, when she is addressed by the teacher. The teacher notices that and starts to direct her questions to Josefa *Josefa, explica pra Ana como é o Adivinha O Que É* [Josefa, explain the riddles activity to Ana] (line 6). Having ensured Josefa's participation, the teacher continues with the guessing activity *O que é o que é?* [What is ... ?] (line 10) with the whole group. As mentioned earlier, Josefa's linguistic repertoire is composed of both English and Portuguese as a result of being born and raised in England and being exposed to Portuguese by her mother from a young age. In addition, Josefa has experienced the unspoken rule of the no-English policy where Portuguese is the main and most valued language in the school. Therefore, it is not surprising that Josefa responds to the teacher's requests in Portuguese in an attempt to present herself as a good learner to her teacher.

In the next example, the teacher (T) starts the riddles game which is open to all the students (Ss). Josefa (J) tries to be first to answer almost all the riddles.

**Example 2**

1T: *O que é o que é que tem uma casa mas não paga aluguel?*
[What is it that has a house but does not pay rent?]

2J: *Eu sei, eu sei. A coisa que tem uma coisa* (inaudible)
[I know, I know. The thing that has a thing (inaudible)]
(many children shouting at the same time)

3T: *O que é que o pai e a mãe têm, mas os filhos não têm?*
[What is it that the father and the mother have but the children don´t?]

4J: *Trabalho.*
[Work]

5T: *O que é que o pai e a mãe têm mas os filhos não têm?*
[What is it that the father and the mother have but the children don´t?]

6J: *Casa.*
[House]

7T: *O quê que tem na mãe, no pai que não tem no filho? Vou escrever aqui, ó, vou dar uma dica bem grande.*
[What is it that there is in the mother, in the father which there isn´t in the son? I'll write here. Look, I'll give you a big clue.]

8J: *Orelha* (laughs)
[Ear]

9S: *Cabelo.*
[Hair]

10T: *O quê que tem nessa palavrinha que tem nessa e não tem nessa?*
[What is there in this word which the other word doesn´t have?]

11J: *A.*

12T: *A letra ´a´! Muito bem, Josefa. Mais um ponto pra você. Uh, Josefa está ganhando com 3 pontos!*
[Letter A! Well done, Josefa. One more point for you. Ooh, Josefa is winning with 3 points!]

The teacher again establishes that Portuguese is the language of the classroom activity by using it in her initial question *O que é o que é que tem uma casa mas não paga aluguel?* [What is it that has a house but does not pay rent?] (line 1). Although it is an open question addressed to the whole class, Josefa tries to answer it immediately *Eu sei, eu sei. A coisa que tem uma coisa* [I know, I know. The thing that has a thing] (line 2). She seems to be trying to ensure that nobody else answers before her and perhaps jeopardises her identity as a good learner. On this occasion, Josefa does not seem to have taken the time to think about her answer and tries to describe the object she has in mind. It is also possible that Josefa does not know the word she is looking for in Portuguese and tries to provide the teacher with the description instead. Moore (2002) discusses how descriptions can be a difficult task for young children and Josefa is not successful in her effort to negotiate meaning in Portuguese. What is interesting on this occasion is that Josefa does not switch to English but sticks to Portuguese in accordance with the teacher's expectations. Her language choice on this occasion serves to reinforce her good learner identity and enhance her positive relationship with the teacher.

Unlike Josefa who is focused on the lesson and eager to use Portuguese with her teacher and classmates, Benedito creates opportunities to have parallel interactions with his best friend during the lesson, situations in which he speaks English (cf Creese *et al*, 2008). In classroom interactions with his teacher and classmates, however, he uses Portuguese, as the next example (3) illustrates.

## Example 3

1T: *O Benedito vai falar pra mim como é que eu escrevo abacaxi.*
[Benedito is going to tell me how I spell pineapple.]

2B: *Eu não quero.*
[I don´t want to]

3T: *Vamo, Benedito!*
[Come on, Benedito]

4B: *Não!*
[No!]

5T: *Eu sei que você sabe.*
[I know you know]

6B: *Não!*
[No!]
(The teacher moves close to him and seems to be whispering to him.)

7T: *Qual é a outra letrinha? 'a'*
[Which is the other letter? ´a´]

8B: *'t'*

9T: *Não. Abacaxi.*
[No. Pineapple]

10B: *'b'*

11T: *Isso! Muito bem.*
[Yes! Well done]
(The teacher goes back to the board and speaks to the whole class.)

12T: *a-ba..e depois, Benedito?*
[pine ... and after, Benedito?]
(Other children volunteer to help out. Benedito keeps silent.)

I observed that Benedito was generally keen to participate in the learning activities. In this extract, however, he refuses to spell the word 'pineapple' in Portuguese to the group. When invited by the teacher (line 1), Benedito refuses to take part, *Eu não quero* [I don't want to] (line 2). Benedito's forceful refusals to spell in public *Não!* [No!] (lines 4 and 6) are in Portuguese. In other words, while Benedito is not being cooperative he is trying to save face and preserve his image as a good learner by using Portuguese. By choosing to speak Portuguese while refusing to participate in the activity, Benedito also signals that he is only uncomfortable with the spelling activity, not with speaking Portuguese itself. The teacher seems to understand this and tries to help him: she approaches Benedito and prompts him by whispering the next letter in his ear (line 7). The teacher's strategy seems to work as Benedito tries to spell the word himself (line 8). As Benedito's answer is wrong, the teacher stays by him and prompts him with the whole word again (line 9). The fact that the teacher is standing close to Benedito seems to make him believe that this is a private exchange as his mistake does not seem to deter him from trying again (line 10). He is then successful in his attempt to spell the word given by the teacher and is praised for his effort (line 11). One would expect Benedito's achievement to motivate him to try to finish spelling the word. However, this does not seem to be the case. As the teacher moves back to the board and asks Benedito to spell the whole word (line 12) he resorts to silence, perhaps in an attempt to protect his image as a good learner by avoiding a situation which could lead him to make mistakes.

The children often participated in speaking activities about typical Brazilian animals and their eating habits, and were then given pictures of animals to colour in. The teacher and the assistant went around and interacted with each child individually in Portuguese. The teacher-pupil interaction was based on the children's colouring activity but triggered other topics too.

Benedito used these activities as an opportunity to interact privately with his classmates in English. The following example is a case in point. On this occasion, one of the boys was throwing his pencils at the other children. The third time this happened, the teacher asked the boy to stop his task and sit on the sofa alone instead of at the table with the other students. The boy obeyed the teacher initially but started to disturb the other children again as soon as the teacher was busy giving individual help to other children. Benedito, however, spots his classmate's conduct and indirectly alerts the teacher.

**Example 4**

1B: I hate this. What about you?

2S: (inaudible)

3B: No, up here. Question, question, question.

4B: (singing aloud) *YYYY tá debaixo da mesa*
[Y is under the table.]

5T: *YYYY, vai pro sofá!*
[Y, go to the sofa!]

In line 1, Benedito addresses one of his classmates in English, the language he considers appropriate for his private conversation with peers, as stated in his interview. This interaction is continued in English (lines 2, 3). However, in line 4, Benedito sings aloud in Portuguese describing what another classmate is doing, *Y tá debaixo da mesa.* [Y is under the table.] It appears that Benedito is making a public statement and, indirectly, directing his utterance at the teacher. Benedito's choice of language proves him right in relation to the appropriateness of his use of Portuguese: he is successful in catching the teacher's attention while presenting himself as a good learner who uses Portuguese appropriately in the classroom. The teacher hears him and reprimands the student who is misbehaving (line 5).

Benedito is not only aware of the difference in status of the two languages in the classroom but he also uses their status difference to achieve his interactional goals. Benedito's goals vary but it can be said that in general he makes language choices depending on whether he considers his conversations to be public or private. He addresses his teacher in Portuguese and his peers in English when in private and in Portuguese when in public interactions, such as whole group activities which involve his teacher or the teacher assistant.

Like Benedito, Antônio, who is older than the other two children and attends level 3, uses Portuguese and English depending on context and participants. However, his language choices do not seem to be as neatly separated as Benedito's. In the example below, Antônio addresses his teacher in English. On this occasion, the teacher has put the lesson on hold because the children have been disruptive and kept talking to each other. The teacher addresses the whole class to point out that their disruptive behaviour will probably affect her intention to allow the children to play outdoors. Antônio attempts to turn the tables by pointing out that although the children were at school on time, they had to wait for about half an hour for the lesson to begin, implying that the teacher was late.

**Example 5**

1T: *A gente ia fazer uma atividade lá fora, mas acho que não vamos mais ter tempo.*
[We were going to have an outdoors activity but I don´t think we are going to have any time for that.]

2A: Yeah, but that was only because we started at twenty-five to ...

3T: *Não entendi nada.*
[I didn't understand anything.]

4S1:*Ele disse ...*
[He (Antônio) said ... ]

5T: *Ele vai falar pra mim.*
[He (Antônio) is going to say it to me.]

6A: *Porque nós ... nós ... ah ... vinte e cinco pras duas.*
[Because we ... we ... ah ... twenty-five to two.]

7T: *Por que?*
[Why?]

Although the teacher uses Portuguese in addressing the whole group, Antônio chooses to speak to her in English when indirectly accusing her of starting the lesson late (line 2). His challenge expressed in English could be seen as particularly risky as the content of his utterance is already loaded. Indeed, the teacher seems to be offended by the remark and particularly by the use of English. Thus, she exercises her authority by feigning lack of understanding and demanding that he repeats his utterance in Portuguese *Não entendi nada* [I didn't understand anything] (line 3), *Ele vai falar pra mim* [He is going to say it to me] (line 5). The teacher's use of Portuguese reminds Antônio of the appropriate language to be used in classroom talk. In an attempt perhaps to mitigate the force of his utterance, Antônio decides to comply with the teacher's request and switches to Portuguese.

In the next example, the teacher and the children are having a geography lesson focusing on the names of the states in Brazil and their capitals. As a follow-up activity, the teacher has asked the students to tell the group about the places they have visited in Brazil, things they have done there and how they liked it. Antônio takes the next turn and chooses to talk about a holiday resort he visited in the Northeast of Brazil.

**Example 6**

A: *Quando eu foi pra Natal eu foi no cachoeiro e tem os os* <u>slides, slides</u>?
*Escorrego. Mas é de ...* <u>rock</u>*..é é de pedras, natural. E você parou no piscina natural lá.*
[When I went to Natal I went to a waterfall with <u>slides, slides</u>? Slides. But it was of ... <u>rock</u> ... of of rocks, natural. And you ended in the natural swimming pool there.]

In his short description, Antônio uses Portuguese as much as he can. However, he uses two words in English, 'slides' and 'rock'. As I mentioned earlier, Antônio's exposure to Portuguese is more limited than that of Josefa and Benedito. Therefore, it could be said that he uses these two English words as sentence fillers because he cannot find the right words to express himself in Portuguese. However, Antônio uses an enquiry tone in the first case and pauses in the second one. These two strategies may indicate that he is not only searching for the right words in Portuguese but also asking for help. Although there is no help from the teacher or any of his classmates, Antônio's strategy works as it enables him to remember the correct words and insert them in his description. Here the two languages are juxtaposed as an integral part of Antônio's learner identity.

## Conclusion

As other chapters in this book have shown (eg Chapters 1, 2, 3 and 12), the children's language choice and identity negotiations reveal an understanding of the different values attached to Portuguese and English. More specifically, the recordings showed that the children mainly interacted with their teachers in Portuguese and with the other children in both languages. They oscillated between the use of Portuguese and English to negotiate one particularly salient identity option, that of a good learner of Portuguese.

To conclude, it is important to highlight the impact the school has on the children's learning experiences and links between their language learning and processes of social identity construction. Indeed, the Brazilian Portuguese school may be the main site where mixed-heritage children interact with other children in the heritage language. For this reason alone, the role of the school in the maintenance of Brazilian Portuguese deserves to be highlighted (see also Chapter 7).

# Part III:
# Policy and practice

# 9

# Teachers' developing theories and practices in Greek Community Schools

*Efstathia Pantazi*

## Introduction

Community schools not only reflect the linguistic and cultural diversity in mainstream society but are a powerful reminder of Britain's failure to meet the needs of the children of different communities who attend them. Linguistic, cultural or religious diversity present challenges for mainstream and community schools alike. One key challenge is to identify the pedagogic approaches that most adequately meet the needs of ethnic minority children.

Communities vary according to the degree their members maintain the heritage language and culture. In some communities the heritage language may be in regular use across domains, while in others assimilationist pressures may have forced the heritage language into retreat, even in the private sphere (Baker, 1996:184). Furthermore, the cultural identities of minority community members, especially those of the second or third generation, tend to be hybrid, seen as a complex amalgam of features of the dominant and the heritage cultures (Bhabha, 1998). Finally, the linguistic and cultural profile of any particular community is bound to change over time.

In terms of pedagogic approaches, the variety and complexity of teaching and learning contexts implies that there cannot be any one best way to address how ethnic minority children should be taught (Hornberger, 2002). As Cochran-Smith and Lytle (1993) wrote about mainstream education: the 'complexity of the tasks faced render global solutions to problems and monolithic strategies for effective teaching impossible' (p63-64). But this can be applied to community education too. Locally tailored approaches are called for, appropriate to the specific needs of the students in a given socio-cultural context. Teachers of ethnic minority children in community schools can develop such approaches because on one hand, teachers are uniquely positioned to gain local knowledge of their minority students' needs (Kincheloe, 2003) and, on the other, they have the potential, under certain conditions, to develop their teaching theories and practices reflectively, '[con-structing] their own questions [and beginning] to develop courses of action that are valid in their local contexts and communities' (Cochran-Smith and Lytle, 1993:63-64).

This chapter explores how a group of teachers in Greek community schools in London developed locally tailored approaches. First, I provide a brief out-line of the Greek community schools and of the teachers who are the focus of this research. Then, drawing on in-depth interview data, I trace the reflective cycle which a group of Greek teachers went through as they modified their understanding of language, culture and identity and their approaches to teaching and learning to accommodate the needs of their pupils in the con-text of the Greek community schools where they taught. I conclude by dis-cussing the implications of their modified approaches for policy and practice.

## Greek community schools

I draw on research conducted in Greek complementary schools in the Greater London area during 2003 to 2006 (Pantazi, 2006, 2008). These schools cater to a large Greek-Cypriot and Greek community, and have been created to help maintain Greek language and culture. The schools operate in the evenings and at weekends and supplement the children's mainstream education.

The children attending classes come from a variety of backgrounds, with some households predominantly speaking Greek, some only English, and others which have one or more bilingual family members and where both languages are in use. Teachers working in the Greek community schools include members of the local community and graduate students from Greece and Cyprus working part time while they complete their studies. However, the majority of teachers are qualified and experienced professionals from Greece and Cyprus on secondment from their countries for five years, and it is this group who participated in the research presented in this chapter.

A series of in-depth interviews were conducted in order to trace how the theories and practices of these teachers developed over the five-year period they taught in the UK. An additional perspective was provided by my own insights since I was also working as a teacher in the schools during the period of the research. All the teachers had had previous experience of working with ethnic minority students including Albanian students in Greek mainstream classrooms, students in experimental intercultural schools in Athens, or students in Greek community schools in countries such as Switzerland or the USA. Many of the teachers had an interest in furthering their understanding of bilingualism and biculturalism through academic study in the UK. Consequently, their developing theories and practices represent informed and considered reactions to the specificities of the particular condition of the Greek schools in the UK.

## Tracing the reflective cycle

When teachers come to the UK from Greece they often experience difficulties in the classroom due to a series of factors: the students' low-level of competence in Greek, their lack of motivation and their own frustration with available textbooks which they perceive as poorly matching the students' competences, learning styles and interests. In these cases there is often a disjuncture between the teachers' expectations and the reality. Such experiences can be described as 'critical incidents'. A critical incident is a shock, possibly a turning point in one's personal or professional biography (Brookfield, 1990; Tripp, 1993; Sikes *et al*, 2001).

Facing difficulties in the classroom, the teachers try to adjust to their new teaching environment by building up local knowledge of the students and their backgrounds. One of the key areas of local knowledge focuses on the pupils' linguistic resources. Nikos (all names are pseudonyms) recalls a particular sentence that one of his students produced during the first lesson: *Ο παπάζ λαλεί οτο* church *την προδευχή* <the priest says the prayer in church>. The sentence contains linguistic elements from standard Greek, the Greek-Cypriot dialect and English. The sentence encapsulates the linguistic diversity in the schools: the students use English in class, rather than exclusively Greek, the level of language use is not as high as the teachers expected and, instead of using standard Greek, most students generally use the Greek-Cypriot dialect.

Teachers quickly become aware that language use within the community is complex. Jorgeos expresses a sentiment common among most of the teachers when he claims that second and third generation students 'have difficulty communicating in Greek'. They realise that, while recently settled families – often those from Greece – continue to use Greek in the home, for many of the second and third generation Greek Cypriots there has been a certain 'language shift' (Paulston, 1977), with English becoming the dominant language in the home.

The picture which emerges from the teachers' descriptions is of a complex form of diglossia within the community. The form of diglossia has changed over generations (see Paulston, 1992), so that Greek is no longer the dominant language for most students. However, there is a sizeable minority who do speak Greek at home, resulting in significant differences in language competence in the classroom. In addition, there is variation in the form of Greek used within the community schools: the dominant variety of Greek spoken by the students is vernacular (Greek-Cypriot dialect), while they are taught standard Greek.

Another important area of local knowledge developed by teachers has to do with their revised understandings of the students' culture and identity. They stress the hybrid nature of the students' cultural identities. As newcomers, similar to their students, teachers also bring with them elements of their home culture, forming a hybrid culture in their new home, influenced by the host country's culture (Bhabha, 1998). However, the teachers identify perceived tensions with respect to the students' cultural identities. Some of the teachers who have worked with Greek communities in other countries (the USA and Switzerland) see a difference with the community in the UK. As Costas puts it 'they want to look and act like English. In Switzerland the Greek elements were more clearly visible'. At the same time, as Michalis acknowledges 'there is a part that belongs there [Greece, Cyprus] ... even if they want to cut themselves off, they can't do it'. In addition, the teachers see ambivalence in some of the students towards learning Greek, which they argue is manifested in their lack of motivation in the community school classes.

Michalis, like many other teachers I interviewed, traces these tensions to pressures in mainstream schools to be monolingual, where there is little or no recognition of the students' heritage culture or language. According to Viki: 'the [mainstream] teachers ... don't know what percentage of the students speaks other languages'. Effectively, the failure to recognise the home culture and language renders such minority community children 'invisible' in the mainstream (Moore, 1999:34; also Chapter 7). This can be seen as a form of 'symbolic violence' (Bourdieu and Passeron, 1977), resulting in 'home/school disarticulation' (Baker, 1997).

Two significant points arise from this. Through coming to appreciate the assimilationist pressures which exist in the mainstream, the teachers see more clearly the gap which the community schools fill. The second point is the intimate link the teachers see between language and identity: that the marginalisation of the Greek language in mainstream schools is central to the tensions some students feel about their cultural identities (see Chapter 6).

As teachers continue to develop their local knowledge, they also begin to distance themselves from powerful discourses both within and beyond the community schools. On the one hand, there is a local discourse within the community schools shared among powerful stakeholders such as head teachers, priests, influential members of school committees and parents, that teachers come to see as a static view of Greek culture (see Chapter 1 and Chapter 3). On the other hand, there is a powerful discourse from Greece, which is reflected in initial teacher training seminars before teachers come to the UK, and in the textbooks supplied by the Greek state. According to this discourse, the mission of community schools is to support the Greek diaspora which spreads across the globe from Australia to Africa and from Argentina to North America. The teachers come to see the assumptions underlying the textbooks and the initial teacher training seminars as out of touch with the complexity of bilingualism and cultural identification in the Anglo-Greek community, ie Greek is not as dominant as it is assumed to be, and the students' culture is more hybrid.

While working in a number of different schools each week over a period of five years, teachers gain rich experience: by becoming more aware of the issues faced by the community school students, they start to modify their teaching practices in order to meet their needs better. As qualified professionals who have chosen to move abroad to work in the community schools, they are motivated to find solutions, and working outside of the rigid curriculum imposed by the Greek state gives them freedom to experiment.

The process through which these changes take place is one in which there is mutual influence between theory and practice. Practice is influenced by 'theories-in-use' (or 'action theories', Schön, 1983) – that is practical knowledge, gradually built up by teachers. Such theories are normally resistant to change, but under certain conditions they can 'give way to a new and different perspective' (Osterman and Kotcamp, 2004:14) and can therefore modify practice. Moreover, as teachers experiment with new classroom approaches, they reflect on their experiences and their theories are further modified. In this setting, then, conditions exist for the teachers to move through a reflective cycle, in which modifications to theory and practice are mutually reinforcing.

## Modified approaches to language teaching

In their interviews, teachers repeatedly take issue with the textbooks used in the community schools, which are produced and supplied by the Greek state. Agni reports that the textbooks are

> very difficult ... [The level] is higher than the level they speak. It presupposes that they speak this language, that the oral tradition survives at home.

When asked to describe an unsuccessful lesson, Demitrius links it with the use of textbooks: 'mostly [in] the first year when I was trying to exhaust the whole textbook. The kids didn't want to follow'. The teachers say that the textbooks use outdated methodologies, unsuited to the students' learning styles. This is because, as Amalia points out, for many years 'things haven't changed [in the community schools], although methods, approaches and pedagogy have developed [elsewhere]'. They realise that there is a mismatch between the students' learning styles (based on the teaching styles they are used to in the mainstream) and the teaching style in the community schools, which is influenced in part by the approach adopted in the textbooks. The teachers find that the students are used to a wider range of materials, and respond better to an approach in which the set text is supplemented with materials which they have produced themselves.

They also emphasise the effectiveness of a range of approaches which move away from static, book-based teaching. These include the use of visual stimuli, computers, music and drama. Miltos highlights the value of visual media: students respond to them well, and images are an effective means of explanation:

> I very often use visual stimuli – whenever I've taken the laptop, and have had the ability to show them pictures of what I'm talking about, or explain with visual representation, I had much better responses and attention!

Teachers find that students respond well to the use of music and drama in the classroom. Concerning the latter, Viki was involved in producing plays in Greek and, comments: 'Do you know how much more Greek you learn in this way? ... The school must be fun as well!' It can be noted here that this range of approaches corresponds to various forms of 'intelligence' posited by Gardner (1993) in his theory of multiple intelligences. The teachers find that by bringing in activities which cater to the more visual (spatial), musical or physical (bodily-kinaesthetic) aspects of the students' personalities, they generate interest and get better results.

Teachers also come to understand that students' expectations are shaped by their learning experiences in the mainstream school. They see, for example, that students respond better to grammar teaching that is embedded in the context of a reading text or some other task, than to one that is explicitly presented. Grammar here is seen to support the lesson rather than being its main focus; further, the emphasis is more on use (communication and the negotiation of meaning) than on structure. All the teachers emphasise the importance of using communicative approaches with these students: 'communication is very important, I believe' (Costas) and 'when everything happens through communication and conversation ... it works over time' (Viki).

When asked to describe successful lessons, the teachers typically recount activities drawing on students' existing knowledge and interests. Michalis recalled a lesson on the Olympic Games that 'was high interest' because the Olympic Games was taking place in Greece that year. They covered the subject for two or three weeks and Michalis felt that project work was the key element that accounted for its success. Summing up his account: 'that's exactly what we have to do: to build on the experience they already have about Greece – through the school, their travels or the family'. Another teacher, Viki, put together a project based around a text she had written about tourism in Greece and Cyprus. The students discussed what they knew from their holidays in Cyprus: 'where they go on holidays, where they swim, which beaches are clean'. The task was then to write this up as an article. Viki accounts for the success of the lesson:

> the elements now are ... they must know something to start with ... When they participate, it's not only me who talks ... They discuss what they're interested in ... [And] because they have to make linkages, they use different tenses – they have to talk about the past, present and future.

Here the teacher draws on the students' own knowledge. It is significant that the lesson is about Cyprus: part of the community's 'funds of knowledge' (Moll, 2000:258). The children from the Greek-Cypriot community have firsthand experience of the island. Importantly, the children are positioned as the 'experts'; the teacher is not Cypriot so they are teaching *her*.

More broadly, both these examples fit very well into the communicative paradigm, in particular the task-based approach (Ellis, 2003): the project was a task, both themes were described as interesting and generated a lot of conversation. It is also clear that these successful community school lessons gave the students opportunities to explore further the Greek and Greek-Cypriot side of their cultural identity. The lessons demonstrate how cultural identity issues can be closely linked to successful language teaching.

A significant commonality between the teachers is that they try to facilitate student engagement by finding bridges between the students' existing understanding and the language they need to acquire. Such attempts to adjust one's language and approach to the needs and level of the learners can be referred to as 'scaffolding' (Wood, Bruner and Ross, 1976) defined as '[ways of] helping students ... to tackle tasks they are interested in but unable to manage alone' (Wells, 2001:89). One example would be by drawing attention to cognates: English words with a Greek root, such as *democracy, chemical, centre* or *telephone*. By focusing on these kinds of language features, students can improve their knowledge and understanding of both languages. Michalis says: 'I explain how the Greek language is used in, for example, medicine, or in the everyday language'. Such an approach rapidly expands students' vocabulary-base, since they will already know many of the English words; it can also increase students' confidence in their ability to progress.

For the teachers, another scaffolding tool is the judicious use of English within the classroom. Although the teachers try to keep classroom talk in Greek as much as possible, they recognise that English can be used to reduce anxiety and sometimes to make learning more effective. Overall, too, the teachers show sensitivity to the actual level of the students' Greek.

## Modified approaches to culture and identity

The teachers see tensions between what students come to understand as Greek culture and their own cultural identities in British mainstream schools. They argue that the ethnocentric nature of the mainstream British curriculum means that there is not much coverage of Greek culture and history. Amelia recalls a lesson in which the students were asking her about Greek history:

> In GCSE they have just three pages on Greek history. They didn't know about antiquity, the Byzantine empire, and the empire of Alexander the Great reaching India at one time ... I was explaining the different periods – to understand the importance of the Greek contribution to human history.

In this instance we can see the role of the community school in providing a space in which the value of students' heritage cultures can be recognised and even celebrated. The teachers see the potential to give students a positive impression of Greek culture, to correct what they see as omissions and distortions by the mainstream. As Costas puts it: 'you can create a love of [Greek] books in the students ... there is a whole world – there's [Greek] literature, there are [Greek] movies, there's a whole [Greek] culture'.

In addition to providing a space in which children's cultural heritage is recognised, these classes can also become fora for identity negotiation. The teachers talk about bringing the students' own experiences into the classroom. As one teacher notes:

> you can show respect for what these children carry from their environment and from the English school – and use it ... the experience of living a hybrid existence. Teachers have to bring in the Cypriot culture, as well as the Greek.

Jorgeos stresses the importance of the teacher trying to understand the complex reality of the students' lives and their identities and the importance of sensitivity towards the heterogeneity existing within the local culture:

> To show them that; 'yes, although I come to teach you Greek, or some things about the Greek culture ... I accept that you live here, that you are an amalgam of cultures and I'm interested to learn from that' ... to help to bring out together what you have. So when you do that they will participate in the lesson and it will be successful. Because what makes a lesson successful is participation.

In this context, the classroom becomes a forum within which cultural identities can be explored by both students and teachers (Giroux, 1998). By drawing on the students' backgrounds during the lesson, teachers help them maintain a secure sense of self where a central aspect of their identities is validated. This also creates the possibility for the negotiation of alternative identity options (Cummins, 2003:54). Furthermore, by giving the students the chance to share their personal experiences during lessons, opportunities are created for meaningful communication in Greek and thus for more satisfactory language lessons.

In the teachers' discourse there is an emphasis on the present, on the living culture as it is experienced in Greece and in the UK. Set against a static, nostalgic view of Greece, teachers feel they bring to the classroom 'the real picture [of Greece] and not Ελληνολατρεία [the image of an idealised Greece]'. They argue that the Greek teachers can make connections between idealised understandings of Greek identity and contemporary ones, between the distant past and the local present. As one teacher puts it: 'we can bridge the gap [and] this must be our aim'. As a result, teachers seek to weave contemporary understandings of Greek culture into language lessons in the community schools. For instance, one teacher was involved in an internet-based project among Greek community schools located in different countries and an English mainstream school. For the community school students, this project presented an opportunity to find out more about aspects of Greek history and culture, and to make links to the present in a collaborative context. According to the teacher who participated in the project, the treatment of culture became 'something dynamic and about the now – about the present'. The teachers make efforts to bring contemporary Greek culture to life for the students. Michalis cites a lesson in which they discussed the high-rise blocks in Athens:

> this is a social issue so we started to discuss why they have these houses. And we started to talk about the περίπτερο [street-corner kiosks] as part of the everyday life, as part of Greek culture ... [and to connect this] to their everyday life.

In this language lesson, Michalis drew on students' own experiences of visiting Greece, and linked the Greek reality to that in the UK. This kind of up-to-date, personalised treatment of culture as an integral part of language teaching also has benefits in terms of increased student motivation.

Another dimension to the teachers' approach is through their work with dance, song, drama and other embodiments of the culture. Eleni, for example, who uses a lot of Greek music in her lessons, argues:

> all these different elements constitute this way of living ... Because this culture is a way of life – that's alive. My approach is that the children have to live it: the children join in, they're part of it.

Having used drama with her Greek-language students, Viki feels that:

> it helps you to understand who you are, your sense of self. ... through the re-telling of the story ... and through the process of direction they learned so many things about their culture and civilisation.

The notion of culture, which informs the teachers' discourse here, is one which stresses the role of participation as a route to understanding. In this sense, culture does not reside only in objects and representations, but also in the bodily processes of perception by which those representations come into being. Culture can be found 'in human practices, situated in people's involvement' as people 'live culturally' rather than 'live in cultures' (Moll, 2000:258). Thus, in the teachers' discourse, forms such as dance, theatre or music are seen as the embodiment of a culture, and a form through which it can be understood.

## Implications for policy and practice

This chapter has shown that when teachers are faced with a reality for which their existing teaching theories has left them unprepared, a process of reflective development can be initiated. This process is empirically grounded: they conduct informal research, initially by building up local knowledge, later through experimenting with new practices. The picture that emerges of the educator is that of a 'knowing subject' (Freire, 1970), constantly learning from the process of teaching and reflecting. Pedagogic knowledge is not something that is handed down; rather it is constructed out of experience, action and reflection (Osterman and Kottkamp, 2004:24). Since classrooms in modern multicultural societies are characterised by their diverse, heterogeneous nature, there are clear advantages in facilitating reflection so that pedagogy is grounded in teachers' own experiences within that setting.

What, then, are the factors which initiate and sustain this process of reflective development? Critical incidents act as triggers, and for this group shifting from mainstream classrooms in Greece to community schools in the UK provoked many such incidents. For a number of the teachers, however, a reflective process had already been initiated when working with bilingual students in Greece. This points to the fact that the reflective development of theories and practices is shaped by the teachers' sense of self, which in turn is shaped by their life experiences and backgrounds (Goodson, 2005:236). It should also be taken into consideration that these teachers had all chosen to work in the UK. This willingness to relocate in order to work in the community schools could explain in part their high level of commitment to improve practice.

However, certain conditions can be provided by policy-makers to facilitate the reflective process. One of these, mentioned many times by the teachers, is to have the time and the space properly to discuss pedagogic practices with colleagues. Another necessary condition is having sufficient freedom to experiment in the classroom (Soin and Flynn, 2005:77). For these teachers, moving from the grip of the national curriculum in Greece to the relative freedom of the community schools provided vital spaces for experimentation and innovation. This finding resonates with an OECD study on educational innovation in 13 countries (Black and Atkin, 1996). As the lead author of the report highlights:

> where matters are interlinked in complex ways, and where one has to be sensitive to the local context in which this complex is situated, then only those who have the freedom of manoeuvre can then turn a good idea into a really effective innovation (Black, 1997:60).

Although this research focuses on the Greek community schools, moderate generalisations (Williams, 2002) can be assumed to apply to teachers working in the community school sector more broadly. One point stressed by the teachers is the importance of building closer links between community schools and the mainstream. Although many of the Greek community schools use classrooms in mainstream schools for their evening and weekend classes, they suffer from a similar invisibility as the students: little cooperation or communication is forthcoming from the mainstream. However, as one teacher puts it: 'the Greek school is part of the education of the student. His education concerns both of us'. Opportunities for teachers in the two systems to visit one another's classes and to discuss issues of mutual concern, more opportunities for the community schools to use the facilities of the mainstream schools (eg computers and other facilities) and to have a more visible presence there, would give this shared responsibility a more concrete form (see Chapter 12).

In terms of teacher education there should be more scope for trainee teachers to visit community schools and learn about this aspect of education (see Chapter 10). As seen above, the shift to working in the community schools prompted a process of reflective development for the Greek teachers. In order to gain an insight into the linguistic, cultural and identity needs of minority community students, it would be extremely useful for initial training or in-service training to incorporate such experiences:

> to move beyond simply knowing about ... multiculturalist practice ... [student teachers] need to take the required steps towards an embodied and corporeal understanding of such practice and an affective investment in such practice at the level of everyday life (McLaren and Torres, 1999:71).

Two further implications arise. Firstly, policy-makers and academics can look to teachers working in multicultural settings as potential contributors to policy, to the material-writing process, and to research, since they have detailed knowledge of specific communities with which they work, and of how to teach them effectively. Further, to have such knowledge built up through reflective processes, policy-makers in both community schools and the mainstream should ensure the necessary conditions exist: primarily, opportunities for dialogue both within the school and externally, eg with academics, together with initiatives to allow teachers to explore different forms of practice and to reflect on their experiences.

# 10

## Developing links between communities, schools and initial teacher training

### *Leena Helavaara Robertson*

And again that was fantastic! I wish all children did something like that with their parents. From walking through the hallway you could see parents doing a lot of different things and even cleaning up; you know getting down and sweeping the floor, clearing up and making food, and making coffee and talking. And that sort of gave me the idea how strong the community part really is. Because all these parents weren't just there. They were there to stay and talk. They were there for the day. (Sabia, final year teacher training student commenting on his visit to a Turkish community language school)

## Introduction

This chapter is based on a Multiverse (TDA) funded research project (Robertson, 2007a). The project aimed to discover how to develop connections between different kinds of learning resources among various groups of people in one part of North London. Uniquely, the project brought together teacher training students, like Sabia (all names are pseudonyms) whom I quote above, Middlesex University, as the local North London Initial Teacher Education (ITE) provider, and two Green Lanes community language schools plus some local primary schools.

Based on a socio-cultural view of learning (Moll *et al*, 1992; Rogoff, 2003), the project involved a small group of final year BA (Hons) ITE students who were training for Key Stages 1 and 2 and had successfully completed their final school practice. They participated in this project by visiting local Turkish and Greek schools as a part of their initial teacher education and being interviewed before and after their visits. During their visits they completed tasks and wrote observations, all of which were collected. The interview transcripts, tasks and observations were shared with participating Turkish and Greek teachers and ITE tutors in order to identify emerging issues. Later, some of the findings were also presented to mainstream primary teachers for discussion.

This chapter begins by summarising the policy background around community cohesion and presenting a brief overview of research that straddles mainstream and complementary schools. It goes on to explore the divergent definitions that emerged during the study about what counts as a community among the different participants (eg teacher training pupils, community school and mainstream teachers). Then, it discusses the teacher training students' shifting perceptions regarding ethnic minority pupils, language learning and achievement. It concludes arguing that a collaborative approach between mainstream and community language schools is a powerful way to shift teacher training students' long held assumptions and perspectives, challenge societal and institutional stereotypes about ethnic minority children, learning and achievement in schools and ultimately help develop community cohesion.

## Policy background and review of the literature

Over many decades the need for developing links between different linguistic and ethnic minority communities and mainstream schools has been highlighted in a number of governmental reports, eg the Bullock Report (DES, 1975), the Swann Report (DES, 1985). Whilst some progress has been made, much more needs to be done. The Race Relations Amendment Act (RRAA) of 2002 (HMSO, 2002) shifted the attention from responding to the needs of ethnic minority groups to promoting good relations between different ethnic groups. This became a duty, in which all public organisations, such as universities and schools, are now expected to engage. Subsequently, a number of government documents have advocated increased collaboration and renewed partnerships between schools and children's families and communities. For example *Excellence and Enjoyment: A strategy for primary schools* (DfES, 2003a) aims to foster strong links with communities, and the same thread of collaboration and community involvement can be found in *Every Child Matters* (DfES, 2003b) and its extended schools agenda. The Education and Inspections Act 2006 introduced a duty to all maintained schools in England to promote community cohesion, and on Ofsted, to report on the ways in which schools engage with this agenda (eg DCSF, 2008). A cohesive community is defined as follows:

- there is a common vision and a sense of belonging for all communities
- the diversity of people's different backgrounds and circumstances is appreciated and positively valued
- those from different backgrounds have similar life opportunities
- strong and positive relationships are being developed between people from different backgrounds in the workplace, in schools and within neighbourhoods

(DfES, 2004, n.p.)

Dyson and Gallannaugh (2008) reviewed research literature in education policy, and identified community cohesion as a fairly recent theme, to judge by the fact that there had not yet been sustained research in this area. Furthermore, theories that govern young children's learning in schools have virtually exclusively focused on mainstream schools rather than community groups' provision and often it is the monolingual, middle class children whose learning processes, experiences and academic progression are viewed as normative (see Conteh *et al*, 2007a for further discussion). Yet, for many children the essential tools for learning are provided by both mainstream and community schools. Many children move between the two parallel classrooms regularly (Robertson, 2006, 2007b), and for many years, and both sets of schools are necessary in becoming bi/multilingual and bi/multiliterate and in developing and maintaining a strong sense of identity.

At present, there is a growing number of studies focusing on mainstream and community language schools. Some have examined learning in community language schools in more detail. Gregory's ground-breaking work in this area (eg Gregory, 1993; Gregory and Williams, 2000; Gregory *et al*, 2004) has explored a range of learning contexts, such as Chinese community language schools and literacy learning in mosques. Hall *et al* (2002) examined community language schools in England and Norway whilst Bhatt *et al* (2004) and Martin *et al* (2007) studied those in Leicester, and Robertson focused on schools and young children in Watford (Robertson, 2006, 2007b). Reay and Mirza (1997) and Mirza and Reay (2000) have discussed the black African-Caribbean supplementary schools in England. Barradas (2007) found a positive correlation between learning in Portuguese community language schools in London and the attainment of English in mainstream schools as measured by the national tests (SATs).

Many of these studies have identified an urgent need to tackle assumptions that surround many ethnic minority pupils' learning within homes and communities, such as parents' perceived lack of interest in their children's education, and the subsequent low expectations of pupils' academic achievement within mainstream schools (see Chapter 11). Authors such as Reay and Mirza (1997), Mirza and Reay (2000), Hall *et al* (2002), Kenner (2004) and Conteh *et al* (2007b) have discussed the deficit-model that continues to linger around multilingual and black minority ethnic (BME) pupils' learning within their communities. The lack of contact and collaboration between schools and communities, between different types of teachers (community and mainstream), between ITE providers, researchers and policymakers, has often been often cited (Hall *et al*, 2002; Kenner, 2004; Conteh *et al*, 2007b) as a contributing factor in the formation of these negative assumptions.

## Setting the scene: the teacher training students and the community schools

Four students, three female and one male volunteered to take part in the study. Sophie, at the age of 21, was one of the youngest students on the whole course, and both her parents had been born in Italy and had arrived in England as children. Sabia, the only male student to take part, was 25 years old and from Ireland. He was also the only one to consider himself bilingual as he spoke both Irish and English. Louise, at the age of 34, regarded herself as a typical London student. Her grandfather had come over from Italy and she had very fond childhood memories of the London Italian community. Mandy, at the age of 47, had lived in different parts of England and London. She had arrived in Britain from the Caribbean at the age of 7.

It is important to emphasise that these students volunteered to take part in the project because they all readily identified with EAL and ethnic minority children. Each one of them mentioned commitment to teaching children and enhancing their experiences. They all disclosed aspects of their personal background whilst talking about their own school practices. They were clearly comfortable with their own identities and backgrounds.

The students expressed a preference to visit community language schools in pairs, and hence two local schools, the East Hills Turkish School and the Green Meadows Greek School, were selected as the most suitable. The two schools operated mainly on Saturdays. They rented their premises from the two mainstream schools East Hills Secondary School and Green Meadows Primary School respectively. The schools' consent was requested via telephone. The visits and tasks were explained, and the head teachers agreed to discuss their schools' involvement with other teachers and parents. The schools' consent was confirmed during a later telephone conversation. After the visits, the Greek and Turkish teachers were involved in discussing and evaluating the teacher training students' tasks and interview transcripts. This was seen as an important part of the project as it established a dialogue between ITE tutors and communities. It also enabled ITE tutors to find out what the schools' and teachers' own agenda might be, and how research could try to address this. Moreover, it provided opportunities to share emerging findings directly with the schools and communities involved.

None of the students had attended or visited community schools before, but all were aware of their existence. Within this project Sabia and Mandy visited East Hills Turkish School and Sophie and Louise visited Green Meadows Greek School. Sophie and Louise observed four separate sessions, two in the morning and two in the afternoon. Mandy and Sabia observed one morning and one afternoon session.

## What is a community?

One of the very first issues to emerge from this project was the lack of shared understanding of what constitutes a community. The word community comes from Latin *communitae* and means 'held in common', but participating students, Greek and Turkish teachers, university tutors and mainstream school teachers all expressed different viewpoints on what exactly holds a group of people together. The term community was at times used to describe the geographical area around a school, as in the neighbourhood or local community, and it included all residents, places of work and amenities. The members of the community were often perceived to have diverse histories, beliefs and values, and consequently they were seen as being part of a diverse community.

When used in this context, the term was not contested, and it had many positive connotations. Louise's description of the Green Lanes area in North London and its community is a good example:

> It's nice to be able to go to those areas because they have kind of adopted, or they have brought their own home culture to our country. So you don't even have to go on a plane to experience these different types of countries. We've got them in our back garden. Which is excellent!

For the Turkish and Greek teachers the term community was first and foremost tightly related to ethnicity and language. The Greek community included everyone in the loosely defined local area who had some kind of well-established link with Greece or Cyprus. It included people who had recently arrived from Greece or Cyprus; for example, a number of the school's teachers were completing Masters or PhD studies and had been in London from six months to three years. It also included those who were of first, second or third generation Greek background and those who were of mixed heritage. It included English parents and people of other ethnicities who were in long-term relationships with Greek people. The Green Meadows Greek School teachers also talked about the role of the school in pulling the community together. The school was established over 25 years ago and had continued to provide a focal point for the community, as the head teacher explained:

> All those years ago, we met some families who had young babies. First they didn't attend the classes. Then, a few years later they started coming and they went through the school. Now they bring their own babies.

Developing the ability to speak, read and write in Greek was important and one of the main aims of the school. However, because many children of the second and third generation preferred to use English which was their dominant language, code-switching and mixing Greek and English were typical practices (see also the previous chapter).

A similar picture emerged in the East Hills Turkish School. This school had been in operation since 1982 and the school continued to provide an important focal point for the community. Here the community members were of Turkish, Cypriot or Kurdish backgrounds and the school welcomed all Turkish people, their partners, children, grandchildren who had lived in the local area for some time as well as those who had recently immigrated to England, including some refugee families of Kurdish origin, and those who had lived there for a short while. The school also provided invaluable informal support in helping new families to find out about housing, health and education in the area.

However, the term 'community' raised questions when used for linguistic or ethnic minority communities. When sharing some of the findings with mainstream school teachers, some head teachers questioned the use of this term. In this context these teachers perceived the concept of community as divisive and unnecessary. They questioned the overall purpose of bringing together one linguistic or ethnic community because they perceived it as 'not inclusive', 'not bringing this group into mainstream schools' and 'kind of, saying it is fine not to belong to the mainstream school'. For them, community involvement with regards to involvement with the ethnic or linguistic community was neither acceptable nor advisable.

The lack of shared understandings about what constitutes community and who is allowed to define it and, therefore, what community involvement might entail, raises some serious questions about the government's intention to encourage collaboration between schools and their communities.

## Teacher trainees' shifting perspectives

There were noticeable differences between the teacher trainees' thoughts before and after the visits, which pointed to certain shifting perspectives. These shifting perspectives included the teacher trainees' perceptions of ethnic minority communities and of community language schools as valuable sites of learning. For example, as the opening quote of this chapter demonstrates, after the visits the students perceived the Turkish and Greek families in more positive terms as they now thought that they actively supported the children's learning. When talking about different ethnic minority communities before the visits, the students' perceptions were those of an outsider – one which had been constructed within and validated by mainstream schools. Even though ethnic minority communities were part of the mainstream schools' general community, before the visits the students did not talk about them from an inclusive perspective. Ethnic minority communities were typically perceived as separate from and outside of the schools' funds of knowledge.

After the visits they were beginning to move towards a more inclusive perspective. They were beginning to see these communities through the community members' own frame of reference. On many occasions they had viewed minority ethnic communities as being outside the norm, but after their visits they began to challenge this. Louise talked about this at length:

> They [children aged around 6 years in the Greek school] had started to form letters and stuff and, I mean it is really intricate language to try to write in. And because we just do the English, to us it really is quite daunting! Because to us it kind of looks really hieroglyphics. And the other children [outside the Greek community] should be able to experience that, the language and the culture, and that would be beneficial. And it would just enhance the whole learning environment. And when you have other children who are from other backgrounds, it just makes it ... I don't know, normal?

They begun to see the two communities from a new perspective as Sabia's recollection of his visit to the Turkish school revealed:

> I stood out like a sore thumb. My colour, my face, just generally. From walking into that environment, I felt I was noticed straight away. They didn't say anything to me, but they were looking at me, as I walked in. I parked my car, probably put it in someone else's space. Then I went in and there were a lot of people that noticed me and initially I appeared as an outsider. You know that fear when you walk in and you think that, gosh, I'm an outsider. And to know that that

happens everywhere. That's how they [Turkish children] must often feel. So that must be a social barrier that children must cross. I think in linking two schools [mainstream and community language schools] in that respect would be good. So that there is a close relationship between what the schools are doing.

The students started to understand the rationale behind the term 'community language school' and talked about the cohesiveness of the community group. They highlighted how the children and adults felt a real sense of belonging to their own communities and how they existed side by side with other communities, all of which were part of the broader North London community. Mandy observed that: 'they were all, yes, so amazing. Such pride. I thought they were all amazing! Dedication. So strong in their identity'. In a similar vein, Sabia observed that:

When the parents [at the Turkish school] came to lessons [ ... ] I asked the teacher whether that person helps in the school. She said no, it's my plumber. He's doing my plumbing. So they trust each other. There is a lot of trust in that place.

The visits had had a direct impact on how the students now viewed their pupils in their teaching practice schools and as a result they had began to challenge their own and their schools' assumptions. They had moved closer to ethnic minority pupils by viewing them from a different, new perspective. Phrases such as 'I never knew ... ' were used time and time again in the interviews after the visits. Sophie was also clear about her own learning and what she would now do differently in her own classroom: 'their strengths, and their languages, you know. You would be able to incorporate into other lessons. It's less scary now. You just think, I'll do that'.

## Challenging the deficit view

Because usually, I know it's not very nice, but when I see an Ofsted report, if a school has loads of EAL children, I think oh, no! It's going to be quite a struggle teaching them. But now I got a totally different view because all the EAL children in my class, in my final school experience were all just so bright, and brighter than the children that were English and born in this country. So I have totally different view of EAL now.

Sophie's frank thoughts, as quoted above, resembled what Sabia, Louise and Mandy also expressed in somewhat more reserved tones. Considering the fact that the four students had volunteered to take part in this project, had expressed a wish to learn more about diversity in schools and were clearly committed to deepening their understanding of all children's learning, their expectations of ethnic minority pupils' achievement were astonishingly low. If this is the case then what kinds of expectations might other students have? Moreover, it is equally important that these low expectations had not been successfully challenged by the university, nor by the mainstream schools. In fact, the students' low expectations of EAL children were routinely reinforced by the mainstream schools' grouping of children into 'ability groups', as Mandy pointed out: 'well, basically, I mean, most of these children [EAL] were put in the lower ability groups'. In the majority of cases, the teacher training students were unable to change any of the seating arrangements or the composition of the ability groups in the teaching practice schools. They had to conform to existing school practices and routines, as Mandy's thoughts about the practice of placing all EAL children in lower ability groups revealed:

> I'm not sure that that's actually right because it's their language that is their problem, not their ability to do, you know, do maths or whatever. So normally I find that they're put right in the low ability group, so I don't know, until they can understand English well.

Withdrawing EAL pupils from the classroom activities and providing additional literacy support on the side can be seen as a form of exclusion reflecting a deep-seated deficit model of EAL in many schools. The community school experience that started to challenge Sophie's perceptions of EAL children and question the deficit view of EAL was a school in Whetstone. The school was located in a wealthy area of North London and the children taught by Sophie were of Japanese, Indian (Gujarati) and Albanian backgrounds.

> In my final school experience I had two Japanese girls, one Indian boy and one Albanian boy. But they were all very high achievers. They were all in top groups, for everything. I don't know, I couldn't just believe, they were EAL but they were the highest achieving in the class, and just totally ... I just always thought that EAL, they would always be underachievers but that was not the case at all. That was a big shock.

After her visits to the Green Meadows Greek School, Sophie continued to reflect on her shifting perspectives and rejected the label EAL completely as it seemed to contain too many negative connotations: 'now, I don't think like that any more. Now I've got it in my head that they are not EAL. They are bilingual!' Louise began to question the need to keep the two languages, English and Greek, separate because she had seen the benefits of children working bilingually:

> Louise: They do say that like, this is my Greek school, and this is my English school, but really ... it is all part of the child's education. Part of their learning. And I do think the children do need to have that acknowledgment. And I think it's us teachers that like to draw the lines.

Interviewer: Yes, because it all happens in the same head?

Louise: Yes, that's it! They don't put one head on and take the other off. And say that this head is English and the other is Greek!

The visits to the community schools had also increased the teacher training students' confidence, as Mandy pointed out:

certainly [I'm more confident] about talking about culture in the classroom, getting them involved and making children aware of different cultures, also maybe asking what a word is in Turkish, asking them to translate a word in Turkish, and maybe have different words on the wall, in different languages, that would be useful.

## Conclusion

Community language schools can play a vital role in developing strong and positive relationships between mainstream schools and people from different backgrounds, thereby playing a central role in developing community cohesion. Teachers from the Green Meadows Greek School and East Hill Turkish School participated in this project by placing the four students in their schools, explaining their schools' histories and practices to the students, and looking through some data and students' tasks. It was evident that the community teachers perceived both participating ITE students and university tutors as having faith in them and their schools. The head teacher of the Greek School also highlighted this point: 'we wish more would come to see what we do. And the more we get to know the mainstream schools' teachers, the better we can support the children'.

This chapter and the research study it was based on suggest that a collaborative approach between mainstream and community language schools can provide a powerful way to shift teacher training student perceptions and thinking. During the project, the four students who visited community language schools began to question some of their own deficit views of children from linguistic minorities and challenge some long-held societal and institutional stereotypes about ethnic minority children. The visits also helped them to raise their expectations of parental engagement in the children's learning. In addition, they began to see the value of building connections between mainstream schools and the communities' own organisations. As Sophie put it: 'yeah, one Saturday morning is not that much, but it could mean so much!' ITE providers clearly miss a valuable opportunity if they do not learn to tap into these resources.

All the students expressed an interest in continuing to visit community schools for a range of different purposes. All talked about organising visits, ie asking community teachers to visit their own classes once they had qualified and in return visiting their children's other schools and classes. Sophie's starting point was the children's potentially challenging behaviour in her own class:

> Yes, like if in my school there are lots like Turkish children, I would probably go ... If they attend a Turkish school, I'll probably attend that school, to see how they get on there. And that like if they're badly behaved in my school, I'd see how they get on there and if they behave a lot better there, then I'd like to see what strategies the teacher is using.

Louise thought about curricular links between the two different schools:

> I do see the potential. To make the links. You know, just to see what kind of curriculum they're teaching and if there are any cross-curricular links between their curriculum and our curriculum.

Overall, the students' experiences revealed an urgent need for schools and ITE providers to define communities and to ensure that the government's intention to increase collaboration between mainstream schools and their communities is successful. There is an urgent need for ITE providers and schools to foster more positive attitudes towards EAL and ethnic minority pupils in order to combat deficit views and low expectations that continue to haunt many learners in schools today. The extended schools agenda must be inclusive of linguistic minorities and ethnic minority communities and their community provision. Indeed, schools that already operate within the mainstream school buildings are ideally placed to show the way forward. As Sabia put it:

> both [community and mainstream school teachers] come together around the extra curricular activities, like community schools, then perhaps they would be willing to meet in the middle. You can develop a lot from there.

# 11

## Linking community and mainstream schools: opportunities and challenges for Portuguese language and culture classes

*Olga Barradas*

I have been teaching Portuguese as a community language in London for over twenty years. Now, for the first time in my teaching experience, I have *alunos-netos*. I call them grandstudents – the children of those who, many years ago, were my own students and attended the classes of *Língua e Cultura Portuguesas* (Portuguese language and culture, henceforth PLC). My former students, whom I knew as children but who themselves are now mothers and fathers, still call me *professora*, as they did then. One of them, Sofia, expressed her concerns that her daughter is becoming less interested in Portuguese. 'If she does not speak Portuguese, how can she speak with the grandmother and the family when we go to visit them in Portugal? She is using Portuguese less and less. She will forget everything!'

When I began teaching in London, in the mid-1980s, teaching in mainstream classrooms focused on topic work, linking various areas of knowledge and exploring overlapping subjects. The National Curriculum was an innovation about to be implemented and a debate raged over its pros and cons. As a community language teacher, there was little contact between my classes and the mainstream classrooms. However, in the school where I taught, due to the openness and initiative of the head teacher I was allowed to withdraw the children from their classroom half an hour before the end of the day in order to start my lesson. This allowed a precious window of contact with some class teachers.

At the time, being able to establish that link with the classroom teachers, even if brief and informal, gave me the chance to identify the main topics being studied during term. I could then find overlapping areas with the PLC curriculum in order to try to adapt my lessons accordingly whenever possible. One example of this was 'The Romans'. In my lessons, I looked at the Roman influence on Portuguese history and culture.

In this way, knowledge was reinforced and the same topic was approached from the point of view of two different cultures. Children could see a direct link between the work that was done in the after-school classes and the day school. They discussed it with their English-speaking peers and boasted about being able to do school work in two languages. And then ... the National Curriculum was implemented. The school day was almost too short for all that had to be done. Teachers had to concentrate all their time and energy on delivering the curriculum. My classes could only start after school hours and any contact with mainstream teachers dissolved into thin air.

## Introduction

Community language classes are an important aspect of children's education and learning. They offer a cultural and educational niche within the wider society. In this chapter, I consider how recent policy initiatives open up possible opportunities as well as present some challenges for the teaching and learning of community languages in general and Portuguese in particular. First, I provide a historical overview of PLC classes to situate my discussion of policy initiatives in a particular community context. Before offering some thoughts for the future of complementary schooling in the UK, I briefly discuss evidence indicating that attendance of PLC classes can positively contribute to the young people's academic experiences and exam results in the mainstream, thereby reinforcing the case for developing links between complementary and mainstream schools.

## PLC classes: a historical overview

PLC classes in the UK started in London in the 1960s. They were organised and paid for by the local community. Parents recruited the teachers, paid for materials and, when necessary, for the cost of hiring the rooms where the classes took place. At the time, Portugal was still in the grip of a dictatorship and many people migrated to escape economic hardship, political persecution or colonial war in Africa. In the 1970s, under the umbrella of the Greater London Council and the Inner London Education Authority, these classes were able to take place in schools, after school hours. The teachers, though, were still paid by the community. It was only in 1976 that the Portuguese Government took on the responsibility for recruiting and paying teachers. Therefore, what started as a grassroots community initiative developed into an organised government funded enterprise. In practical terms, this has meant that all the teachers are fully qualified professionals and that, as a rule, classes take place in mainstream school classrooms.

However, if 40 years ago parents wanted their children to learn Portuguese and maintain a cultural link with the home country in order one day to return to Portugal, that aim is less clear nowadays. What some have referred to as the myth of return is no longer a myth. Given the ease of travel, many Portuguese families maintain strong links with both the UK and Portugal. At the same time, the current economic climate means that more people are migrating to the UK. This time it is not only unskilled labourers but also skilled people and professionals. Therefore, whilst a third generation of the Portuguese community is beginning to emerge, the characteristics of a second and first generation migrant community are still present.

With regard to their organisation, PLC classes are now under the umbrella of *Instituto Camões*, a Portuguese government agency responsible for implementing cultural and educational policy abroad (http://www.instituto-camoes.pt/missao-do-instituto-camoes/instituto-camoess-mission-2.html). The role of Portuguese as a crucial element in maintaining Portuguese identity and an affective link across diasporic communities has been recognised in legislation (Presidência do Conselho de Ministros, 2008). Nevertheless, there are still close links between PLC classes and the communities they serve. This is evidenced in the setting up of the Association of Portuguese Teachers and Parents in London. Similar to the first PLC classes, this is a grass roots community initiative and it involves local representatives. This Association may, in time, come to fulfill an important role as a community voice liaising between mainstream schools and PLC classes.

## Opportunities for collaboration between schools and communities

In recent years, the UK has seen large numbers of immigrants enter the country, particularly from Eastern European countries that have joined the European Union since 2004. BBC News reported that, according to the Institute for Public Policy Research, even areas which had not traditionally attracted migrants such as Scotland and South-West England had noticed a 'significant' influx (BBC, 2008a), with the number of migrants coming to the UK for a year or more rising to a record level in the 12 months to mid-2007 (BBC, 2008b). Notwithstanding the fact that the employment rate amongst these migrants was higher than the average of the UK-born workers and that they tended to work four hours longer per week (BBC, 2008a), the House of Commons' Communities and Local Government Committee reported 'significant public anxiety' that 'cannot simply be dismissed as expressions of racist or xenophobic sentiments'. This was related to 'practical concerns', such as overcrowded accommodation and pressure on public services, which included the number of newly arrived EAL children in schools (House of Commons, 2008).

Pointing the finger at migrant communities is not new. In 2002, David Blunkett, then Home Secretary, suggested that immigrants should speak English in their own homes (Blunkett, 2002). The Portuguese community, like many others, also felt the social pressure to abandon Portuguese in favour of English. Before Portugal joined the then EEC in order to enter the country, migrants were forced to go through strict, often humiliating and cruel bureaucratic procedures. Regulations often forced families to separate and work restrictions created a feeling of not being free in the UK.

More recent incidents affecting majority-minority community relations, such as those which occurred in the Thetford area in 2004 and even in Jersey, where the Portuguese community has been established for decades, have highlighted social problems associated with migration (EDP24, 2004; BBC, 2004). Inevitably, these experiences of exclusion contribute to shape the identity of the community and of its members (Barradas, 2004) and they filter through to the school environment. These tensions in minority-majority relations are encapsulated in two young people's comments below:

> Joana: At school, we have girls that say: 'Oh! You're Portuguese'. At school there's a group of Spanish girls, one year above us, ( ... ), and there's the proper English people. So they start interfering. Because they're different. Because you're different, you can't be liked. You speak another language ...

> Paulo: Sometimes, there are (school) colleagues that- they say: 'go and speak your rubbish Portuguese, here it is English, this is the English land. It is not Portuguese'. (Barradas, 2004: 286)

Schools are strategically positioned in society to influence community relations. As such, they can take on a pivotal role. In view of global changes and increased migration, and following national and international disturbances in 2001 and 2005 (London bombings), community cohesion became an important focus of legislation and official guidance (see also previous chapter). Since September 2007, schools have a new duty to promote community cohesion, by promoting equality of opportunity and inclusion for different groups through a 'strong respect for diversity, they also have a role in promoting shared values and encouraging their pupils to actively engage with others to understand what they all hold in common' (DCSF, 2007). Schools, taking into account the nature of their population and location, are to do this by focusing on three strands that have been acknowledged by researchers and official publications to play an important role in the academic success of bilingual/bicultural students:

- Teaching, learning and curriculum: The importance of valuing diversity, promoting and strengthening cultural awareness and identity so that language minority students can become bicultural as well as bilingual and working 'ardently on improving the social support system to engage students socially' (Rumberger and Larson, 1998:88)

- Equity and excellence: Focusing on outcomes, thoroughly monitoring pupil and school attainment by ethnicity and deploying teaching support and resources successfully to raise achievement, which also raises questions about expectations, class setting and exclusion processes

- Engagement and extended services: Including links with different schools and communities, the provision of extended services and opportunities for pupils, families and the wider community to take part in activities and receive services which build positive interaction and achievement for all groups. However, creating careful links with the local community, establishing effective and realistic communication with families from different cultures implies the allocation of staff and resources

All three strands carry important implications for teacher training and recruitment (Lytle, 1990; Blair *et al*, 1998; DfES, 2007).While promoting community cohesion, schools must also respect and promote cultural diversity. Yet, the report of the *Curriculum Review Diversity and Citizenship* (The Ajegbo Report) (DfES, 2007) identifies several factors that may deter the promotion of diversity in schools. Two of these factors are:

- not all school leaders have bought in fully to the imperative of education for diversity for all schools, in every location, and its priority is too low to be effective

- links with the community – a rich resource for education for diversity – are often tenuous or non-existent (DfES, 2007:25)

The Ajegbo Report (DfES, 2007) points to the importance of a flexible approach to curriculum design that involves teachers and pupils across all key stages. It suggests that education for diversity should be viewed from a whole curriculum focus, with cross-subject topics and areas of study, drawing on pupils' experiences to create meaningful, relevant and effective learning. In particular,

> with a whole-curriculum focus ( ... ) the outcome could be much richer: if a school were to study migration and settlement patterns in their local area through subjects such as Geography and Citizenship, for example, using an investigation/enquiry approach, a viable curriculum initiative could be to link with Maths to provide relevant data analysis and with English to use texts exploring people's various experiences of migration. (DfES, 2007:45)

Importantly, the report provides the following recommendation: 'in planning for extended school provision, schools should seek to make contact with as wide a range of diverse community groups as possible, including supplementary schools' (DfES, 2007:10). Both the *Curriculum Review Diversity and Citizenship* (DfES, 2007) and the *Guidance on the Duty to Promote Community Cohesion* (DCSF, 2007) emphasise the need for education for diversity and links with the community served by the school: '[u]nless schools anchor their education for diversity within their local context, they risk tokenism rather than a practical solution, scratching the surface instead of exploring opportunities' (DfES, 2007:54).

The Extended Schools Programme has been suggested as a way to strengthen links between mainstream and complementary schools by creating partnerships with 'local 'supplementary schools', which provide a cultural education for a community alongside helping pupils with academic studies' (DfES, 2007:57). The main services which the Extended Schools Programme provides for are:

- study support
- childcare and activities for young people
- parenting support
- swift and easy referral to specialist services
- community access (DfES, 2006)

The latter includes 'opening up school ICT, sports and arts facilities to the local community beyond the school day, where appropriate and providing adult learning' (DfES, 2006). Access to continuing education would be particularly important for the Portuguese community in the UK, identified in a social profile of the British workforce by country of birth as early school leavers, at age 16. When Bernardo, a young person attending PLC classes, was asked about his parents' educational experiences, he said the following:

Bernardo: My mum, my mum, I think she also left [school] early. Also, she had me when she was 16 years old and she left school to look after me. They want me to continue with my studies and that I get a good job. Because my father left school very early. He left when he was 16. And I think he doesn't want me to do that. If I can continue studying then I will not leave at 16, I can do a bit more. (Barradas, 2004)

Parental attitudes towards their own education can affect the way they support their child's education. In an analysis of these attitudes, all parents of children attending Portuguese classes, unlike those parents whose children did not attend, indicated recognition of the role played by their low academic qualifications in limiting opportunities later in life (Barradas, 2004). If we expect parents to be involved in their children's education, at an age when the use of online resources is an essential part of the teaching and learning process, they must be given access to these basic skills.

## Some challenges

While the aforementioned policy initiatives may potentially have positive implications for collaboration between schools and communities, there are at least three challenges that need to be addressed. The first has to do with invisibility of complementary school teachers in mainstream schools. In the case of PLC classes, even though they take place in mainstream classrooms, they start after the end of the school day and there is no contact between community language teachers and their mainstream colleagues.

PLC classes are not alone. Martin *et al* (2004), reporting on a study of complementary schools in Leicester, indicate that 'over 50 per cent of the schools in the survey say they never have contact with state schools, colleges and universities' (p9).

Closer links between community and mainstream schools can increase the possibilities for collaboration as well as the sharing of expertise and resources. Community language teachers could offer mainstream schools their knowledge of the community and represent a valuable resource in the development of a whole curriculum approach and cross-subject topics, as put forward in the *Curriculum Review Diversity and Citizenship* (DfES, 2007, see also Chapter 9). This would contribute to improving students' attainment and allow a meaningful link with parents and the community. In the case of PLC classes, recent research has shown that parental expectations and involvement are a powerful driving force to children's academic success (Barradas and Chen, 2008).

Establishing close links between PLC classes and mainstream schools would be straightforward in the schools where PLC classes are only for the pupils attending the school in question. As stated in the website of the *Coordenação do Ensino Português* (2009), such links 'help[s] build cooperative/constructive relationships with schools, facilitating the teaching process and the integration of pupils/parents and Portuguese teachers into the school community'.

The close-knit links that are forged also lead children to confide problems, such as bullying, that affect them during the school day and beyond. A strong link with the community would be of particular use to those secondary schools where there may be problems of disaffection. An investigation into Portuguese students who had fallen through the net of school pastoral care, truanting and abandoning school, reported a breakdown in home/school communication. Parents who did not speak English or were not confident enough to contact the school relied exclusively on their truanting children to establish a link with the school. Thus, a situation of reversed authority was created, where parents depended on children to be able to fulfill their parental role (Barradas, 2000).

Portuguese language and culture teachers can play a pivotal role in communication between mainstream schools, the students and their families. Parents' evenings in Portuguese language and culture classes are regularly used as an opportunity to discuss information received from mainstream schools and to ask teachers for advice on how to proceed with school matters. Teachers can be a source of information and advice for both parents and students. Personal and family problems that impact on children's emotional well-being are often shared with teachers. Amongst parents, support networks are developed and information about schools is regularly exchanged.

A second challenge is securing funding for complementary schools, as mainstream schools can still charge for the use of their facilities, even as part of the Extended Schools Programme. In the case of Portuguese classes where qualified teachers are paid for by the Portuguese government and classes already take place in mainstream classrooms, the introduction of the Extended Schools Programme does not appear to make a significant difference. Although the DfES recognises that schools can benefit from a closer relationship with complementary schools, it is not clear how these schools will benefit if they will still have to pay for the use of the classrooms or, indeed, why they should have to pay fees in the first place when they provide a service not only to a particular ethno-linguistic community but also to the student body more generally. Nevertheless, it has been acknowledged by government officials such as Lord Adonis that '[t]here is a strong case for school premises to be made available to *bona fide* supplementary schools at no or reduced cost' (Education Guardian, 2006).

A case could be made for Portuguese classes to fall within the schools' delegated budget share if we consider the model offered by DfES (2006), as highlighted in Figure 1 below. The classes are for students attending full-time education. They include both the pupils attending the host school and others. In several locations, only the school's own pupils attend Portuguese classes. They offer direct support to some areas of the curriculum, particularly linguistic knowledge, academic content and skills and, as I will discuss in the next section, they increase academic achievement and parental involvement in mainstream schools too.

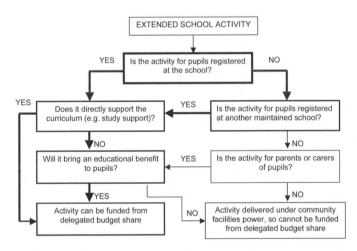

**Figure 1: A case for complementary school classes to be funded from the schools' delegated budget  (Adapted from DfES, 2006:45)**

For Portuguese classes, then,  a case could be made for funding from the delegated budget. As teachers are paid by the Portuguese government, this could take the form of free use of the facilities.

The establishment of closer ties between complementary and mainstream schools, however, raises a third challenge: who decides the content and teaching methodology of PLC classes? There are dissenting voices alerting us to the dangers of state funding. Seddon *et al* (2006) quote the Charity Commission's warning that an 'increased co-operation increases charities' reliance upon the state for fundraising and, in turn, creates a potential risk to charities' independence' (RR7: The Independence of Charities from the State, section 2). The authors also point out that schemes such as the then Resource Unit for Supplementary and Mother Tongue Schools' awards, now part of ContinYou, if enforced as compulsory rather than voluntary, may create a 'regulated environment [that] could stifle the freedom and independence that ... is one of the hallmarks and greatest assets of the sector' (Seddon *et al*, 2006:11). Although acknowledging that many useful links have been established between supplementary schools and local authorities and even central government agencies, it also alerts us to the possible dangers that may come out from this relationship.

In its website, ContinYou indicates the advantages for supplementary schools adopting the NRC Quality Framework. According to the Quality Framework, there do not appear to be any direct benefits for complementary schools in terms of supporting teachers' professional development and curriculum innovation, although there is a mention of the role of local authorities in 'ensur[ing] teaching quality in supplementary schools that they support'. Rather, the focus of the Quality Framework for complementary schools seems to be on the micro-management of schools and accountability of funds (see extract below from the section *Who Benefits from the Quality Framework? (*Contin You, 2009):

- **Supplementary schools** that aim for a Quality Framework Award will gain satisfaction from the fact that their voluntary work is being publicly recognised, and can use the framework to strengthen their services. Schools may also use the framework to gain publicity, funding or opportunities for partnership

- **... Local authorities** will find that the Quality Framework helps them to ensure minimum standards of management and teaching quality in supplementary schools that they support, including those that they would like to commission to provide extended services

- **Mainstream schools** and other partners will know that systems of good practice are in place, and that the supplementary school is working within a culture of self-evaluation and improvement. Quality Framework Awards can be used as evidence for Ofsted and Joint Area Reviews

The perceived benefits for complementary/supplementary schools from the Quality Framework need to be read in the light of Seddon *et al*'s (2006) comment that:

if it were to become a government licensed provider of resource material and consultative inspection, ContinYou would start to take on a relationship similar to that which Ofsted had with independent schools a few years ago: offering optional (but highly recommended) inspections. More recently, that relationship has undergone a subtle shift to become mandatory rather than optional at great cost to educational diversity (p13).

## PLC classes and academic attainment

As many chapters in this book demonstrate, community language classes have much more to offer to those who attend them than just heritage language learning. Despite the absence of formal links or direct cooperation with mainstream classrooms, they can have a strong and measurable impact on pupils' academic achievement. In a study comparing the academic attainment in mainstream education of Portuguese students attending PLC classes and those not attending those classes, Barradas (2004) found a clear difference in favour of the former. The students who attended Portuguese classes consistently outperformed non-attending children throughout all the four Key Stages. The children attending Portuguese classes achieved better grades from KS1 (7 year olds) onwards and this advantage extended to all four Key Stages of compulsory education. They achieved significantly higher academic results than children not attending these classes. The difference was striking at the end of KS4 when children attending Portuguese classes were five times more likely to attain five or more GCSEs grades A* to C than children who did not (see Figure 2) (Barradas, 2007:97).

Interestingly, parental attitudes also proved to be important. Barradas (2004) found that the way parents viewed their own education and their plans for the future affected the children's attendance throughout their schooling, from age 7 to when children completed compulsory education. Parents were

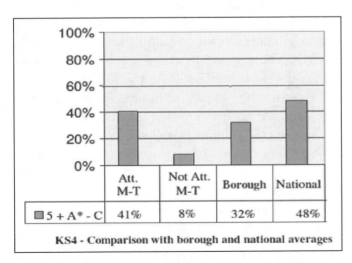

| | Att. M-T | Not Att. M-T | Borough | National |
|---|---|---|---|---|
| ■ 5 + A* - C | 41% | 8% | 32% | 48% |

KS4 - Comparison with borough and national averages

**Figure 2: Portuguese students' attainment at KS4**

crucial in deciding whether or not their children would attend Portuguese classes. Although their jobs often forced them to work long hours, they organised their working life in a way that enabled them to take their children to Portuguese classes. Parents' intention of returning to Portugal coupled with an awareness of the low value of their own academic qualifications and skills provided the impetus to make their children aware of the need for academic success and for maintaining their cultural heritage. Positive parental attitudes, therefore, appeared to have contributed to the high academic expectations they had for their children and to the promotion of inter-generational contact.

It is estimated that around 3,000 to 5,000 supplementary schools are currently offering provision in England (DCSF, 2008). At the time of writing, the DCSF has commissioned a new study on the contribution made by supplementary schools to the education sector and their impact on attainment (2008). This will add to a growing body of research already available which shows that children who develop their multilingual skills by continuing to develop linguistic skills in their mother tongue and by learning through their mother tongue, have an advantage over other children. These advantages relate not only to academic development, English literacy and metalinguistic skills (eg Thomas and Collier, 2002; Kenner, 2004; Sneddon, 2007) but also to aspects of their identity and social development (Souza, 2008) and cognitive skills (Cummins, 1984 and 2000).

## Looking into the future

Exciting times lie ahead for community language schools. Recent policy initiatives have started to recognise the important role community language schools play in maintaining and developing a wealth of knowledge and linguistic diversity in the UK. At a time when foreign language teaching in mainstream secondary education appears to be declining, the '[p]rogression rates from GCSE to A level are considerably higher in relation to community language learning than modern language learning' (McPake *et al*, 2007). According to the same authors 'investing in community languages is likely to produce good returns, in the form of a substantial proportion achieving university entrance level competence'. Community language schools are, therefore, contributing directly to mainstream schools results in languages exams at GCSE and A-Level. In the case of GCSE Portuguese, for instance, students who attend PLC classes tend to achieve grades in the A* to B range.

For PLC classes, presently going through changes in their organisation, this moment offers an opportunity to listen to community representatives and to define clear objectives for the future, both in terms of community needs and in the promotion of Portuguese as a language of choice in schools. However, integrating the teaching of Portuguese into the mainstream school day may carry the danger that instead of Portuguese Language and Culture these classes become simply language lessons with some intercultural knowledge, losing the close links with the local community. This could reduce parental involvement, a crucial characteristic in their present format. PLC classes are about much more than language exams (Barradas, 2004). They are a means of improvement in terms of academic results and linguistic knowledge that can be transferred to mainstream education and translated into future opportunities. They represent a whole family investment with returns in better family relationships, parental involvement in the child's education and higher expectations.

Crucially, they are also an instrument for identity and cultural transmission. Parents want their children to recognise the value of Portuguese culture and, therefore, their own (parents') cultural knowledge. These parents, unlike those whose children do not attend Portuguese classes, are more resistant to pressures from mainstream society to accept English language and culture as the only way of achieving academic success, as the following interview exerpt with one of the children's mothers reveals:

> I think it's [attending PLC classes] good for them, isn't it? At least, so as not to forget and to learn everything about our country. This is not our country. For me, I think it is good for them. I came here and I enrolled them, because, even though they are not yet of full age, I think that it is important for them to know Portuguese. (Barradas, 2004)

For complementary schools more generally, the potential opportunities offered by recent policy initiatives can only be of true benefit to those schools which can improve their management as well as maintain their individuality. Unless schools stand firm in their objectives, in their eagerness to improve what exists and make the most of limited resources, they may succumb to bureaucratic pressures to conform to a particular vision of education and lose the close links with the communities they serve. Twenty years ago I tried to establish links between PLC classes and mainstream classes in one school. It was not possible to do it then. We may now have reached a point where we can take this step forward and create a meaningful partnership. If that happens, it will be a happy day for children like Sofia's daughter.

# 12

## Making links across complementary and mainstream classrooms for primary children and their teachers

*Jean Conteh*

### Introduction

In this closing chapter, I argue that issues of identity and belonging are crucial to the ways that children make links between their learning in complementary and mainstream settings. Their relationships with their teachers are a vital element of their sense of belonging and their success in their different learning contexts. In order to make progress in constructing what are becoming termed 'bilingual pedagogies', aimed to enhance learning for so-called EAL learners, we need to take account of the implications of this.

I support this argument with findings from ongoing ethnographic research in Bradford, a large, former industrial multilingual city in the north of England. The research comprises observations and interviews with children and their parents, carried out over the past five years in a complementary Saturday class, along with a small, funded project where I worked with a group of bilingual teachers as co-researchers to interview mainstream bilingual teachers, some of whom also worked in complementary classes.

I begin by illustrating some of the children's and parents' views and move, through discussion of the teachers' experiences and perspectives, to raise issues for policy and practice, particularly for the education of primary teachers – both mainstream and complementary – and their professional development.

## Making transitions from complementary to mainstream learning – a counting story

Sameena, aged 8, firmly believes that her knowledge of the numbers in Punjabi helps her to do maths in her mainstream class. In the extract below, she is describing to me during an interview how she counts in Punjabi to help herself answer her Year 3 class teacher's hot mental questions at the start of the daily maths lesson:

> We had to count in fives, so I did it in my head in Punjabi then I said it out in English ... Eek, do, teen, cha (one, two three, four) ... twenty-five ... chey, saat, aat, nor (six, seven, eight, nine) ... Thirty ... Eek, do, teen, cha ... . thirty-five ...

In trying to demonstrate how the counting in Punjabi is going on silently in her head while the performance of the English numbers is producing the answers her teacher requires, she varies the pitch of her voice, almost whispering when she says the numbers in Punjabi and saying those in English aloud. She repeats the counting from one to four and then from six to nine in Punjabi, saying the relevant number in English in between, and always keeping the numbers in both languages in sequential order. In this way, she accomplishes the task set by the teacher of counting upwards in fives from 25 to 50 (in English).

In her skilled performance, she could be said to be illustrating the phenomenon of code switching, common to bilingual speakers. But many researchers and teachers have somewhat equivocal views about this way of describing the crossing of linguistic boundaries (Conteh, 2007b:467). The notion of switching does not perhaps do justice to the nature of the feat that Sameena is actually accomplishing. Other writers are finding more illuminative words to describe the way she is creatively and holistically using all her language resources at the same time to solve the problem set by her teacher. Kenner (2004:44) would say that she is displaying 'simultaneous bilingualism' as she 'integrate[s] and synthesise[s] her linguistic resources' to succeed at the maths task. Researchers such as Garcia (2007:xiii) might suggest that she is demonstrating 'translanguaging', a concept fully examined by Creese and Blackledge (2009:8-9).

Sameena, unaware of these debates, is focused on finding the answer to her teacher's questions. She has worked out a strategy for herself that gets the job done satisfactorily. In doing so, it could be argued, she provides a demonstration of Creese and Blackledge's (2009:18-19) depiction of translanguaging as: 'the speaker uses her languages in a pedagogic context to make meaning, transmit information, and perform identities using the linguistic signs at her disposal to connect with her audience in community engagement' (see also Chapter 1).

The idea of performing identities is clearly a significant one for Sameena in terms of her achievement and of the positive ways she is finding to make links between her complementary and mainstream learning experiences. There is no doubt that it is important to her to be seen as a successful pupil in both mainstream and complementary contexts. And she does this, in different ways, by using the 'translanguaging' strategy she has devised. She gets the answers right in mainstream class, earning recognition from the teacher, and is justly proud of it. When she enthusiastically and vividly explains the strategy she used to her complementary class teacher, she receives praise for that, too. She believes that the way she worked out how to count in fives helped her to reach the required level in her KS1 Maths SATs, which she had done a few weeks previously.

At the time she told her story, Sameena was attending a complementary class where her teachers were aiming to develop what they call a 'bilingual peda-gogy' as an explicit means towards raising the achievements and academic potential of pupils whose language and cultural backgrounds they share and who they strongly believe are disadvantaged by the monolingual mainstream system in which they are learning. The bilingual teachers believe that by recognising and valuing all the languages which pupils bring to their learning, and supporting them in their use of them, they can raise their self-esteem, deepen their understanding of the content, concepts and skills in the National Curriculum and help to raise their achievements in mainstream school (see Chapter 9).

Perhaps the influence of these empowering beliefs, underpinning what she had learnt about language in the complementary class, had something to do with Sameena's self-confidence to find a way to use Punjabi alongside English in the mainstream maths activity. No one explicitly guided her in working out her strategy. To Sameena's knowledge, her mainstream class teacher had no idea of what she was doing: she could not count in Punjabi and was probably not aware that Sameena herself could do so. Neither was she aware that Sameena was attending a complementary class in which she was mediating bilingually the same knowledge content and concepts that she was faced with in her mainstream class.

## Complementary classes, community investment and mainstream achievement

The complementary class Sameena was attending is one of over 70 that exist in the multilingual city of Bradford. Like many cities in Britain, Bradford is home to a diverse range of language communities, many of which have for over 50 years sought to maintain their heritage languages and cultures through operating classes and schools to teach their children to read and write in their mother tongues.

As other chapters in this book show, the aims of heritage language maintenance are common in complementary learning settings and links with mainstream schools, in terms of sharing information about curriculum and pedagogy, are rare. But the bilingual class attended by Sameena is different. It explicitly sets out to make links with mainstream learning.

In doing so, it has parallels, in its aims and goals, with a school in Leeds described by Hall *et al* (2002) in a comparative study of four complementary schools, two in Leeds and two in Oslo, Norway. Defining this school as 'supplementary mainstream', Hall *et al* report that its founders are 'acutely conscious of racism and discrimination in mainstream schools', and aim to 'create a supportive mechanism in the community to rise above the discrimination faced by Pakistani pupils in mainstream schools' (p406). There are differences between this and Sameena's class, not least in the more inclusive discourses employed in the Bradford class to talk about mainstream schools (perhaps because the teachers themselves work in both contexts). Also, the teachers in the Leeds school do not seem to share the perceptions of the teachers in the Bradford class of the need to develop a particular pedagogy promoting language-rich teaching and learning interactions. But the hope and aim that the teachers of both classes share for their pupils are that they will make links between their learning in complementary and mainstream settings, and that this will contribute to raising their self-confidence and hence their achievements in national assessments.

The teachers in both settings also share the perception that their pupils are not able to achieve their highest potential in their mainstream classrooms, a conclusion endorsed by Hall *et al* who see the problems as systemic, rather than down to individual teachers: 'it is arguable that the mainstream system is geared to assume deficits in students while the supplementary school locates and teaches to strengths' (p414). In contrast with the cultures of exclusion and low expectation that the parents and teachers perceive in mainstream schools, Hall *et al* provide powerful evidence for the 'sense of solidarity' that they alike gain from being part of a community-based school (p409). Indeed, in the view of the researchers, the prime benefit of the schools is that they 'imbue(s) (its) their participants with a sense of belonging to a community that supports them practically, socially, emotionally and spiritually' (p409-410).

This, they argue, is more important for promoting self-confidence and the potential to succeed than the actual content of the teaching:

> Whether the curriculum focus of the school is mother tongue teaching or mainstream school subject learning, or a combination of curricular foci, the underlying principle in operation is the same – support through strong ethnic identity and community attachment (p410).

Hall *et al* comment further on the way that teachers in the schools they visited see themselves as 'giving something back' to their communities in return for the benefits they enjoy as community members (p410). The teachers' abiding memories of the negative effects on them, as pupils, of the low expectations of their own mainstream teachers motivates them strongly to wish to prevent their own pupils from going through the experiences they themselves suffered. This casts them, according to Hall *et al*, quoting Giroux (1989), as 'transformative intellectuals' and wins them 'considerable gratitude and respect' from both their pupils and their parents (see also Chapter 9). It also matches one of the key findings of the recent, DfES-funded, research project into the perceptions of status and professionalism of ethnic minority mainstream teachers (Cunningham and Hargreaves, 2007). It was found that the 'overarching reason' for their decisions to enter the teaching profession was to 'serve their community' and to 'act as role models for all pupils but particularly for minority ethnic pupils who may be at risk of under-achieving' (p2).

The teachers of the classes researched by Hall *et al* are clearly held in high esteem by parents and pupils alike. Awareness of the value of links between schools, families and communities in promoting success for their pupils is strong. It mirrors the recognition, identified in interviews with bilingual mainstream teachers, of the importance of positive relationships between themselves and ethnic minority parents in schools (Conteh, 2007b:465, also Chapter 10). It is also reflected in the ways in which parents connected with the Bradford bilingual class talk about their teachers.

One mother spoke happily of the way her 7-year old son, who was beginning to be thought to have 'learning problems' in mainstream school, talked 'in a loud voice' with pleasure and enthusiasm of activities he had done in the bilingual class and of how much he liked his teacher. The mother believed that her son had developed greater confidence in mainstream school after attending the bilingual class. She also made the important point, in terms of identity, that it was beneficial for her son to hear his teacher speaking in his mother tongue, something that did not happen in his mainstream school.

The children, when asked about what they gained from the bilingual classes, had some interesting things to say about links with family and community. They spoke about how their parents liked the fact that they had begun to speak more Punjabi at home, and of the ways it helped them to communicate with family in Pakistan. One of the boys went on to talk about the mosque school he attended, linking it with both the bilingual class and the mainstream school in his assertion that they all provided different but equally important facets of knowledge. However, he declared, it was in the complementary contexts that he learned 'manners' and 'pride in your own language', which he valued very highly. He ended his contribution by expressing fervently the opinion that 'mosque and school should be together'.

## Bilingualism: policy, practice and teacher education in primary schools

The long history of contradictions in educational policy in England relating to the needs of bilingual learners is beginning to be well documented (eg Conteh *et al*, 2007b:2-8). Awareness of the lack of recognition of home languages and identities in language policies for mainstream schools, and the negative implications of this, is a common thread running through discussions of complementary and mainstream learning.

The resulting systemic failure to understand and meet the needs of bilingual learners is not restricted to England. Hall *et al* quote the words of a teacher in a community-based school in Oslo: 'the Government does not understand the situation of our children. The state school authorities do not respect the background of our children ... the system functions to discriminate against our children' (p412). Speaking of Denmark, Jørgensen and Quist (in Auer and Wei, 2007) describe the lengthy arguments that took place nationally about the place of minority languages in education. These, they suggest, may have served to emphasise the importance of different languages in children's learning, but in the end made no material difference to what actually happened in schools. They sum up the outcomes in terms that could equally relate to the links between research and practice in England, asserting that 'in this respect Denmark is probably typical of industrialised societies in which scholarship recommends multilingualism, and decision makers strive to maintain monolingualism' (p163).

But as Conteh *et al* (2007b:8-9) go on to show in their historical survey of language education policy in England, it can be argued that research is slowly beginning to influence policy, at some level at least. This can be seen particularly related to primary language pedagogy and primary teacher education. A range of initiatives, all instigated by the DfES/DCSF, such as the *Aiming High* and the *Excellence and Enjoyment* range of resources, as well as the KS2 Languages Strategy, which is intended to introduce the teaching of so-called Modern Foreign Languages (MFL) in primary schools through a skills-based approach, aiming to 'familiarise children with strategies which they can apply to the learning of any language' (DfES, 2005:9) is beginning to promote a new story about language and learning in classrooms. Primary teachers are being encouraged through these means to see language diversity as a positive resource for learning, and to view speaking and learning other languages besides English as an asset, something to be celebrated and used positively in their teaching.

Kenner and Hickey (2008) report several government-led projects (eg Catlow, p158-160; Kirsch, p145-157) which promote constructive approaches to language and learning in mainstream primary schools in England, and from which, they suggest, we are beginning to see positive outcomes.

Teacher education programmes aimed at training specialists in MFL are springing up and, besides doing their job of training language teachers, are providing small numbers of newly-qualified primary teachers (NQTs) with important insights into language and learning on which they will surely build in their careers. In her conclusion, Kirsch (2008) makes the important point, reinforced by the Head of Government Initiatives at the Training and Development Agency for Schools (the TDA, the government agency in England for teachers' ITT and CPD), that 'Primary Language students tend to be more reflective and critical than student teachers in general, and to think about learning and teaching differently' (p149).

Such initiatives are, however, as yet far from the norm in teacher education in England. Despite the growth in provision for teaching MFL on primary ITT courses and the ever-present imperative to develop understanding of the needs of pupils learning EAL, the vast majority of primary NQTs do not have opportunities during their training to consider the role of language in children's learning in principled and coherent ways. The standards required of NQTs (TDA, 2007), along with the ways in which courses have historically been organised and taught, make it very difficult on most PGCE courses to provide holistic approaches to considering language and language education. Most primary teachers currently working in mainstream classrooms in England have had little opportunity in their professional development to develop principled understandings about language and learning. Languages on ITT courses and afterwards in CPD come in unnecessary and restricting boxes, each with its separate label: Literacy, MFL, EAL and so on. Current standards for the teaching of the core subject of English (or, as it is usually cast in school, Literacy, which comes along with its own atomised model of language teaching) and for preparing students to meet the needs of the group of learners categorised with the EAL label are not integrated in any way (TDA, 2007). All of those which relate directly to language are presented quite separately from the only standard (Q18), which states that NQTs need to 'understand how children and young people develop and that the progress and well-being of learners are affected by a range of developmental, social, religious, ethnic, cultural and linguistic influences'. To make matters worse, all these aspects of initial training are usually discretely mediated on courses by separate tutors.

It is not surprising and no fault of theirs, then, that most NQTs begin their first jobs as primary teachers with no real principled understanding of the role of language and culture in learning, and little idea of the ways in which languages can be linked in order to provide the best learning experiences for all their pupils. There is an urgent need for a move in primary teacher education, towards constructing courses which help new teachers to develop clear conceptual understandings of the links between language, culture and learning and with a well-defined model of what could be defined as 'primary language teaching', which should be about promoting 'the generic skills for learning, and about developing the positive values, attitudes and awareness that the language learning experience can provide' (Conteh, 2008:20).

## Bilingual teachers in complementary and mainstream contexts: language, culture and identity

The teachers in the Bradford class, like the vast majority of teachers in complementary settings in England, are bilingual. In previous writing (Conteh, 2007b:466-469; Conteh, 2007a:129-132), I have shown examples of their bilingual classroom interactions with their pupils, and represented their own views of their language and discourse choices in their teaching. Here is how one teacher described the way she is developing a bilingual pedagogy with her pupils:

> Arifa said that she felt very relaxed about using both languages in the way she did and that she found it easier in some ways than teaching in English only as

she could use whichever came most easily as the discourse progressed. She felt that she did not really make conscious moment-by-moment decisions about when to switch from one to the other, but that she had decided on a few key purposes and kept these in mind (Conteh, 2007b:468)

The seamless way in which she is able to move from one language to another and the naturalness of it to her in her teaching is more evidence of translanguaging, which is demonstrated, not only in the way that she mediates her languages, but also in the way she performs as a bilingual teacher. Through this, she claims the classroom space and places 'bilingualism in the centre' (Conteh, 2007a:196).

All of this supports Heller's argument for the need to move away from the idea of languages as codes (2007:6), and to replace it 'with the idea of linguistic resources which are socially distributed, organised certainly by speakers individually and collectively, but which do not necessarily ever have to correspond to some closed and wholly describable system'.

Such a proposition clearly, as Heller goes on to demonstrate, has powerful implications for language policy and practice in all language learning contexts. It disrupts conventional ideas of how different languages can best be taught and, more radically, calls into question ways in which languages have been labelled and boxed up separately through the history of policy formation and reproduction in England. And when bilingual teachers move from complementary to mainstream contexts, the potential disruption is even greater.

Roberts, in Auer and Wei (2007:415), warns of the need to be aware of 'the communicative ecology of the workplace and the subjectivities that sustain it'. Primary classrooms have their own distinctive hierarchies and tensions (Conteh, 2007a:188), and are just as prone as other workplaces to influences from prevailing social and cultural pressures which constrain bilingual teachers in using their language resources: they, like their pupils, 'understand very quickly that the school is an English-only zone' (Cummins, 2005:590). When bilingual teachers talk about their work in mainstream primary classrooms, they readily express some of the frustrations of the ways they perceive their professional identities are fragmented by the monolingualising ethos of their workplace contexts, as this extract from a long interview with a bilingual mainstream teacher reveals:

Q.  What are your views about using different languages in the classroom?

A.  Oh, they're very very crucial, I feel strongly about that, about using different languages, it's just ... I become .. not resentful ... I just become a bit annoyed 'cos we do have bilingual teachers and being of the similar culture as the children in the schools that we're teaching .. I just feel that the bilingual teachers are not being supported enough ... monolingual teachers tend to think they know better than bilingual teachers, how to teach the kids ... and lots of times I will hear, 'oh, well they're not doing well in English language because they've got no experience, well I resent that because at the end of the day, how can bilingual children, you know, from Pakistan, India, Bangladesh, and various countries, how can they acquire a white middle-class experience, which is what the white teachers are touting for? When we are Asians, and we have a host of experiences, as you well know, that you can tap into, I do resent that, and I do feel that the children are put down because of that ... yes, the English language ... I'm a bilingual ... you know student and they're always saying 'oh their English isn't good enough, well ... my own brother went to Cambridge for English, and we came from Pakistan ..

Q.   So, you think ... certainly, so you don't think .. feel that the benefits of being bilingual are really appreciated?

A.   No ... no, they're not, I mean I use bilingualism a lot and I feel that the children do appreciate that and ... I don't know somehow, but their behaviour changes, ... they're much more accepting towards you because you're identifying their identity, their culture ... you're at one with the children ...

Within the frustrations and the anger, there is recognition of the strength and potential of bilingualism in the classroom, and awareness that there is an important role to be played in identity performance; most importantly, as another teacher suggests, with the children:

I think my background influences me to the extent that I can relate to those children who feel they have dual identities and are unsure about where they belong (a Pakistani-heritage teacher working in a school with a high proportion of African-Caribbean heritage pupils)

and also, as most teachers interviewed suggested, with the parents:

... Asian parents I found are much more welcoming of me ... because I think they've realised that me being ... Asian is actually motivating ... a lot of their kids want to do better and also think that I have ... in a sense ... more loyalty ... towards them and their children's achievements in some sense ... so they've actually been a lot more welcoming (a Pakistani-heritage teacher working in a school where almost all the pupils share a similar language and cultural background)

and, indeed, with the whole community of the school:

... I think the children and the staff and the school do benefit from having an Asian teacher at that particular school ... I think my qualities that I bring in to that particular school do open their mind into thinking that it's not just them, there is more out there ... but sometimes I do feel as though I carry the world to that particular school ... (A Pakistani-heritage teacher in a majority-white school)

Gussin Paley (1979:139) has written about the importance of being 'seen exactly as we are and to be accepted and valued'. This is especially so for bilingual teachers in complementary and mainstream classrooms in England, who are complex, sometimes uncertain and ambivalent, very much aware of the contradictions to be faced. Martin-Jones and Saxena (1995, 1996) and Bourne (2001) have shown how the long-established discourse practices of primary classrooms conspire to 'contain' bilingualism and to cast any bilingual adults who appear there inevitably in the role of 'support'. Bilingual student teachers and NQTs express their anger about not being regarded as 'proper' teachers at all, but perceived as classroom assistants, support workers, even cleaners. Paradoxically, at the same time they are expected to mediate positive messages from official documentation (eg DfES, 2006) which cast their bilingualism as a positive asset in the classroom, and encourage them to use their bilingual skills to help their pupils to learn.

Such contradictory experiences are reflected in Dwyer's (2000) findings about the everyday dilemmas of young British South Asian Muslim women in their articulations of their diasporic identities. These challenge the assumptions of dominant discourses, just as can the presence of bilingual teachers in mainstream primary classrooms. But at the same time, they open up the possibility of alternative identity constructions which offer the potential for greater freedom. Other recent research into teacher socialisation and professional identity (eg Roberts, 2000) has found that ambivalence and duality of experience is a significant issue. Perhaps all teachers, in their different ways, are faced with the need to negotiate competing identities and ideas of what it means to be a teacher, and research into the experiences of bilingual teachers in both complementary and mainstream contexts may well illuminate issues of teacher professionalism which have relevance and application to teachers more generally.

### Thinking differently about language and learning
A focus on culture and identity has the potential to shift our thinking about ways of promoting links between children's learning in complementary and mainstream contexts. If we place the teachers and the learners at the centre

of our concerns instead of the languages being taught and learnt, our pre-occupations change. Garcia (2007:xiii) suggests that, to develop pedagogies informed by the concept of translanguaging, 'we must observe closely the way in which people use language and base our pedagogical practices on that use, and not on what the school system says are valuable practices'. We need to begin to see the aim of teaching as being for each learner to acquire, in the ways most suited to her or himself, the skills to mediate and develop the range of linguistic resources at their disposal in order to increase both those resources themselves and their potential for social interaction. In discussing language policy and teacher education, we need to move beyond ideo-logically framed and loaded terminology such as 'Modern Foreign Language', 'Community language', 'English as an additional language' and the rest. As Heller suggests:

> What emerges now is a sense of bilingualism as only one perspective on a more complex set of practices which draw on linguistic resources which have been conventionally thought of as belonging to separate linguistic systems, be-cause of our own dominant ideologies of language, but which may more fruit-fully be understood as sets of resources called into play by social actors, under social and historical conditions which both constrain and make possible the social reproduction of existing conventions and relations, as well as the produc-tion of new ones. (2007:15)

What teachers need in their training and professional development is to be helped to understand and analyse their own linguistic resources and the strategies they have used in their own learning, so that they can then under-stand how children might approach the task of developing their repertoires of linguistic resources. And the same is true whether it is a monolingual child learning the school language of Literacy, an EAL learner developing confi-dence in English, a child in a complementary setting learning their heritage language or any KS2 pupil learning the new language which is now their entitlement. In this way, teachers will develop understanding of what is essentially good pedagogy for all pupils in all classrooms.

# References

Ahmad, F (2006) British Muslim perceptions and opinions on news coverage of September 11. *Journal of Ethnic and Migration Studies* 32(6) 961-982

Anderson, B (1983) *Imagined Communities*. London: Verso

Ang, I (1994) On not speaking Chinese: postmodern ethnicity and the politics of diaspora. *New Formations* 24 1-18

Ang, I (1998) Can one say no to Chineseness? Pushing the limits of the diasporic paradigm. *Boundary* 2, 25 (3) 223-242

Ang, I (2001) *On Not Speaking Chinese: Living between Asia and the West*. New York: Routledge

Anthias, F (2001) New hybridities, old concepts: the limits of 'culture'. *Ethnic and Racial Studies 24(4) 619-641*

Anthias, F and Yuval-Davis, N (1992) *Racialised Boundaries*. London: Routledge

Anwar, M (1979) *The Myth of Return: Pakistanis in Britain*. UK: Heinemann

Archer, L and Francis, B (2007) *Understanding Minority Ethnic Achievement: race, gender, class and 'success'*. London: Routledge

Archer, L, Francis, B and Mau, A (forthcoming) The culture project: diasporic negotiations of ethnicity, identity and culture among teachers, pupils and parents in Chinese language schools. *Oxford Review of Education*

Archer, L, Francis, B and Mau, A (forthcoming) 'Boring and stressful' or 'ideal' learning spaces? Pupils' constructions of teaching and learning in Chinese supplementary schools. *Research Papers in Education*

Arthur, J. (2003) Baro Afkaaga Hooyo! A case of Somali literacy teaching in Liverpool. *International Journal of Bilingual Education and Bilingualism* 6(3-4) 253-266

Auer, P and Wei, L (eds) (2007) *Handbook of Multilingualism and Multilingual Communication*. Berlin and New York: Mouton de Gruyter

Bailey, B (2007) Heterglossia and boundaries. In M. Heller (ed) *Bilingualism: a Social Approach*. Basingstoke: Palgrave

Baker, B (1997) Anthropology and teacher preparation. *Queensland Journal of Educational Research* 15(2) 41-58

Baker, C (1996) *Foundations of Bilingual Education and Bilingualism* (2nd Ed). Clevedon: Multilingual Matters

Barradas, O (2000) Now you see them, now you don't: Portuguese students, social inclusion and academic attainment. *Goldsmiths Journal of Education* 3(1) 2-13

Barradas O (2004) Portuguese students in London schools: Patterns of participation in community language classes and patterns of educational achievement. Unpublished doctoral dissertation. Goldsmiths College, University of London

Barradas, O (2007) Learning Portuguese: a tale of two worlds. In J. Conteh, P. Martin and L.H. Robertson (eds) Multilingual Learning Stories from Schools and Communities in Britain. Stoke-On-Trent: Trentham

Barradas, O and Chen, Y (2008) How Portuguese and Chinese community schools support educational achievement. In C. Kenner and T. Hickey (eds) Multilingual Europe Diversity and Learning. Stoke-On-Trent: Trentham

Baumann, R (2000) Language, identity and performance. Pragmatics 10(1) 1-5

BBC (2004) Arrests made after England exit http://news.bbc.co.uk/1/hi/world/europe/jersey/3835043.stm (last accessed 05/09)

BBC (2008a) EU migrants settling across UK. http://news.bbc.co.uk/go/pr/fr/-/1/hi/uk/7373552.stm (last accessed 01/09)

BBC (2008b) Drop in East European migration. http://news.bbc.co.uk/go/pr/fr/-/1/hi/uk/7574061.stm (last accessed 01/09)

Bernstein, B (2000) Symbolic Control and Identity: Theory, Research, Critique (revised edition) Oxford: Rowman and Littlefield Publishers

Bezemer, J (2008) Displaying orientation in the classroom: students' multimodal responses to teacher instructions. Linguistics and Education 19 166-178

Bhabha, H (1998) Culture's in between. In D. Bennett (ed) Multicultural States: rethinking difference and identity. London: Routledge

Bhatia, S and Ram, A (2001) Locating the dialogical self in the age of transnational migrations, border crossings and diasporas. Culture and Psychology 7(3) 297-309

Bhatia, S and Ram, A (2004) Culture, hybridity, and the dialogical self: cases from the South Asian diaspora. Mind, Culture and Activity 11(3) 224-240

Bhatt, A, Bhojani, N, Creese, A and Martin, P (2004) Occasional Paper 18: Complementary and mainstream schooling: a case for reciprocity? National Association for Language Development In Curriculum (NALDIC)

Black, P (1997) Ideology, evidence and the raising of standards. In J. Dillon and M. Maguire (eds) Becoming a Teacher: issues in secondary education. Buckingham: Open University Press

Black, P and Atkin, JM (1996) Changing the Subject? Innovations in science, maths and technology education (OECD review of educational innovation) London: Routledge in association with OECD

Blackledge, A and Creese, A (2009) Multilingualism: a critical perspective. London: Continuum

Blackledge, A and Creese, A with Baraç, T, Bhatt, A, Hamid, S, Li Wei, Lytra, V, Martin, P, Wu, C-J, and Yağcıoğlu-Ali, D (2008) Contesting 'language' as 'heritage': negotiation of identities in late modernity. Applied Linguistics 29(4) 533-554

Blackledge, A and Creese A with Baraç, T, Bhatt, A, Hamid, S, Li Wei, Lytra, V, Martin, P, Wu, C-J, and Yağcıoğlu-Ali D (forthcoming) Meaning making as dialogic process: official and carnival lives in the language classroom. Journal of Language, Identity and Education

Blair, M and Bourne, J with Coffin, C, Creese A. and Kenner, C (1998). Making the Difference: teaching and learning strategies in successful multi-ethnic schools. Research Briefs. Research Report No. 59. Suffolk: DfEE Publications

Block, David (2008) On the appropriateness of the metaphor of loss. In P. Tan and R. Rubdy (eds) Language as Commodity. London: Continuum

Blunkett, D (2002) Integration with diversity: globalisation and the renewal of democracy and civil society. In Rethinking Britishness. The Foreign Policy Centre. (Reproduced as part of the Observer Comment Extra 'What does citizenship mean today?' http://observer.guardian.co.uk/race/story/0,11255,792231,00.html (last accessed 06/09)

Borooah, VK (2005) Caste, inequality, and poverty in India. *Review of Development Economics* 9(3) 399-414

Borooah, VK, Dubey, A and Iyer, S (2007) The effectiveness of jobs reservation: caste, religion and economic status in India. *Development and Change* 38(3) p423-445

Bourdieu, P and Darbel, A (1991) *The Love of Art. European museums and their public.* London, Polity Press

Bourdieu, P and Passeron, J-C (1977) *Reproduction in Education, Society and Culture.* London and Beverly Hills: Sage

Bourne, J (2001) Doing 'what comes naturally': how the discourses and routines of teachers' practice constrain opportunities for bilingual support in UK primary schools. *Language and Education* 15(4) 250-268

Brookfield, S (1990) *Becoming a critically reflective teacher.* San Francisco: Jossey-Bass Inc

Catlow J (2008) Excellence and enjoyment: learning and teaching for bilingual children in the primary years. In C. Kenner and T. Hickey (eds) *Multilingual Europe: diversity and learning.* Stoke-on-Trent: Trentham

Census 2001. London: Office for National Statistics. http://www.statistics.gov.uk/census2001/census2001.asp (last accessed 06/09)

Chow, H (2004) *Heritage Language Learning and Ethnic Identity Maintenance: a case study of Chinese-Canadian adolescents.* Regina: University of Regina

Chun, A. (1996) Fuck Chineseness: on the ambiguities of ethnicity as culture as identity. *Boundary* 2 23(2) 111-138

CILT (The National Centre for Languages) (2008a) *Our Languages.* http://www.ourlanguages.org.uk (last accessed 15/09)

CILT (The National Centre for Languages) (2008b) *Shpresa case study.* http://www.ourlanguages.org.uk/working/case_studies/CaseStudy137 (last accessed 08/09)

Cochran-Smith, M and Lytle, S (1993) *Inside/Outside: teacher research and knowledge.* New York: Teachers College Press

Conteh (2007a) Bilingualism in mainstream primary classrooms in England. In Z. Hua, P. Seedhouse, Li Wei and V. Cook (eds) *Language Learning and Teaching as Social Interaction.* Basingstoke: Palgrave Macmillan

Conteh, J (2007b) Opening doors to success in multilingual classrooms: bilingualism, codeswitching and the professional identities of 'ethnic minority' primary teachers. *Language and Education* 21(6) p457-472

Conteh, J (2008) 'Miss, can you speak French?' linking 'MFL', 'EAL' and 'English' in primary language teaching. *Race Equality Teaching* 27 (1) 17-20

Conteh, J, Martin, P and Robertson, LH (eds) (2007a) *Multilingual Learning Stories from Schools and Communities in Britain.* Stoke-on-Trent: Trentham

Conteh, J, Martin, P and Robertson, LH (2007b) Multilingual learning stories in schools and communities in Britain: an overview of issues and debates. In J. Conteh, P. Martin, and LH, Robertson (eds) *Multilingual Learning Stories in Schools and Communities in Britain.* Stoke-On-Trent: Trentham.

ContinYou (2009) Quality Framework for Supplementary Schools http://www.continyou.org.uk/what_we_do/children_and_young_people/supplementary_education/quality_framework (last accessed 12/08)

Coordenação do Ensino Português (2009) Portuguese Education Department – What is the Portuguese Education Department? http://e-portugues.co.uk/?page_id=129 (last accessed 05/09)

Creese, A, Bhatt, A, Bhojani, N, and Martin, P (2006). Multicultural, heritage and learner identities in complementary schools. *Language and Education* 20(1) 23-43

Creese, A and Martin, P (2006). Interaction in complementary school contexts: developing identities of choice – an introduction. *Language and Education* 20(1) 1-4

Creese, A, Wu, C-J and Li Wei (2007) *Investigating Multilingualism in Chinese Complementary schools in Manchester.* University of Birmingham

Creese, A, Baraç, T, Bhatt, A, Blackledge, A, Hamid, S, Li Wei, Lytra, V, Martin, P, Wu, C-J, and Yağcıoğlu-Ali, D (2008) *Investigating Multilingualism in Complementary Schools in Four Communities* (final report). University of Birmingham http://www.esrcsocietytoday.ac.uk/esrcinfocentre/viewawardpage.aspx?awardnumber=RES-000-23-1180 (last accessed 06/09)

Creese, A, Bhatt, A, Bhojani, N and Martin, P (2008) Fieldnotes in team ethnography: researching complementary schools. *Qualitative Research* 8(2) 223-242

Creese, A and Blackledge, A (in press) Translanguaging in the bilingual classroom: a pedagogy for learning and teaching. *Modern Language Journal*

Cummins, J (1984) *Bilingualism and Special Education: issues in assessment and pedagogy.* Clevedon: Multilingual Matters

Cummins, J (1986) Empowering minority students: a framework for intervention. *Harvard Educational Review* 56 (1) 18-36

Cummins, J (1996) *Negotiating Identities: education for empowerment in a diverse society.* Ontario, CA: California Association for Bilingual Education

Cummins, J (2000) *Language, Power and Pedagogy: bilingual children in the crossfire.* Clevedon: Multilingual Matters

Cummins, J (2003) Challenging the construction of difference as deficit: where are identity, intellect, imagination, and power in the new regime of truth? In P. Trifonas (ed) *Pedagogies of Difference: rethinking education for social change.* New York: Routledge/Falmer

Cummins, J (2005) A proposal for action: strategies for recognizing heritage language competence as a learning resource within the mainstream classroom. *The Modern Language Journal* 89 585-592

Cummins, J, Bismilla, V, Chow, P, Cohen, S, Giampapa, F, Leoni, L, Sandhu, P, and Sastri, P (2006) *ELL Students Speak for Themselves: identity texts and literacy engagement in multilingual classrooms* http://www.curriculum.org/secretariat/files/ELLidentityTexts.pdf (last accessed 05/08)

Cunningham, M and Hargreaves, L (2007) *Minority Ethnic Teachers' Professional Experiences: evidence from the teacher status project.* DfES Research Report RR 853.

Curdt-Christiansen, XL (2008) Reading the world through words: cultural themes in heritage Chinese language textbooks. *Language and Education* 22 (2) 95-113

Department of Education and Science (DES) (1975) *A Language For Life* (The Bullock Report). London: HMSO

Department of Education and Science (DES) (1985) *Education for All* (The Swann Report). London: HMSO

Department for Education and Skills (DfES) (2002) *Languages for All: languages for life.* London: DfES

Department for Education and Skills (DfES) (2003a) *Excellence and Enjoyment: a strategy for primary schools.* Nottingham: DfES Publications

Department for Education and Skills (DfES) (2003b) *Every Child Matters, Change for Children: making it happen, working together for children, young people and families.* Nottingham: DfES Publications

Department for Education and Skills (DfES) (2004) *Community Cohesion Standards for Schools.* http://www.standards.dfes.gov.uk/pdf/commcohesion.pdf (last accessed 07/07)

Department for Education and Skills (DfES) (2005) *The Key Stage 2 Framework for Languages.* http://www.standards.dfes.gov.uk/primary/features/languages/ (last accessed 12/2008)

Department for Education and Skills (DfES) (2005) *Extended Schools: access to opportunities and services for all.* London: DfES

Department for Education and Skills (DfES) (2006) *Planning and Funding Extended Schools: a guide for schools, local authorities and their partner organisations* http://publications.teachernet. gov.uk/default.aspx?PageFunction=productdetails&PageMode=publications&ProductId=DFES-0472-2006& (last accessed 05/09)

Department for Education and Skills (DfES) (2006) *Excellence and Enjoyment: learning and teaching for bilingual pupils in the primary years.* Ref: 0013-2006PCK-EN

Department for Children, Schools and Families (DCSF) (2007) *Guidance on the Duty to Promote Community Cohesion.* London: DCSF http://www.teachernet.gov.uk/_doc/11635/Guidance%20on %20the%20duty%20to%20promote%20community%20cohesion%20pdf.pdf (last accessed 04/09)

Department for Education and Skills (DfES) (2007) *Curriculum Review Diversity and Citizenship* (Ajegbo Report) http://publications.teachernet.gov.uk/eOrderingDownload/DfES_Diversity_&_ Citizenship.pdf (last accessed 01/09)

Department for Children, Schools and Families (DCSF) (2008) Programme of research 2008116 DCSF: The Impact of supplementary schools on pupils' attainment: an investigation into what factors contribute to educational improvements http://www.dcsf.gov.uk/research/programmeof research/projectinformation.cfm?projectId=15599&keyword=2008116&keywordlist1=0&keywordlis t2=0&keywordlist3=0&andor=or&type=0&resultspage=1 (last accessed 06/09)

Department for Children, Schools and Families (DCSF) (2008) *Extended Schools Subsidy Funding for Economically Disadvantaged Children and Young People A guide to the 2008-09 pathfinder* http://www.teachernet.gov.uk/_doc/12687/final_Extended_schoo_28C8E9.doc.pdf (last accessed 01/09)

Dien, FSD (2000) The evolving nature of self-identity across four levels of history. *Human Development* 43(1) 1-18

Dunn, J (1989) The family as an educational environment in the pre-school years. In C.W. Desforges (eds) *Early Childhood Education. The British Journal of Educational Psychology* Monograph Series No. 4, Scottish Academic Press

Dyson, A and Gallannaugh, F (2008) School-level actions to promote community cohesion: a scoping map. In A. Dyson and F. Gallannaugh (eds) *Research Evidence in Education Library.* London: EPPI-Centre, Social Science Research Unit, Institute of Education, University of London. Online: http://eppi.ioe.ac.uk/cms/Default.aspx?tabid=2416&language=en-US (last accessed 04/09)

Dwyer, C (2000) Negotiating diasporic identities: young British South Asian Muslim women. *Women's Studies International Forum* 23(4) 475-486

*EDP24* (2004) Violence Flares as England Crashes Out. http://www.edp24.co.uk/content/edp24/ news/story.aspx?brand=EDPOnline&category=News&tBrand=edponline&tCategory=news&itemid =NOED25%20Jun%202004%2009%3A14%3A17%3A020 (last accessed 05/09)

*Education Guardian* (2006) Supporting Role 26/04/2006 http://education.guardian.co.uk/schools/ comment/story/0,,1761723,00.html (last accessed 12/08)

EEC (1977) *Council Directive on the Education of Children of Migrant Workers.* 77/486/EEC

Ellis, R (2003) *Task-Based Language Learning and Teaching.* Oxford: Oxford University Press

Erickson, F (2000) Qualitative methods. In R.L. Linn and F. Erickson (eds) *Research in Teaching and Learning* Vol. 2. New York: Macmillan

Evans, Y, Wills, J, Datta, K, Herbert, J, McIlwaine, C, May, J, de Araújo, JO, França, AC, França, AP (2007) *Brazilians in London: a report for the strangers into the citizens campaign.* Department of Geography, Queen Mary, University of London

Ferdman, M B (2000) 'Why am I who I am?' constructing the cultural self in multicultural perspective. *Human Development* 43(1) 19-23

Flewitt, R. S (2005) Using multimodal analysis to unravel a silent child's learning. *Early Childhood Practice: The Journal for Multi-Professional Partnerships* 7(2) 5-16

Flick, U (2000) Episodic interviewing. In M.W. Bauer and G. Gaskell (eds) *Qualitative Researching with Text, Image and Sound: a practical handbook.* London: Sage Publications

Foucault, M (1972) *The History of Sexuality: Volume 1.* London: Penguin Books

Foucault, M (1980) *Power/Knowledge Selected Interviews and Other Writings, 1972-1977.* New York: Pantheon

Francis, B., Archer, L. and Mau, A. (2008) *British-Chinese Pupils' Identities, Achievement and Complementary schooling: Executive Report.* London: Roehampton University

Francis, B., Archer, L and Mau, A (2009) Language as capital, or language as identity? Chinese complementary school pupils' perspectives on the purposes and benefits of complementary schools. *British Educational Research Journal* 35 (4)

Freire, P (1970) *Pedagogy of the Oppressed.* New York: Herder and Herder

García, O. (2005). Positioning heritage languages in the United States. *The Modern Language Journal* 89(4) 601-605

García, O (2007). Foreword. In S. Makoni and A. Pennycook (eds) *Disinventing and Reconstituting Languages.* Clevedon: Multilingual Matters

García O (2009) *Bilingual Education in the 21st Century: a global perspective.* Oxford: Blackwell

Gardner, H (1993) *Multiple Intelligences: the theory in practice.* New York: Basic Books

Giroux, HA (1989) *Schooling for Democracy: critical pedagogy in the modern age.* London: Routledge

Giroux, H (1992) Resisting difference: cultural studies and the discourse of critical pedagogy. In L. Grossberg, C. Nelson and P. Treichler (eds) *Cultural Studies.* New York: Routledge

Giroux, H (1998) The politics of national identity and the pedagogy of multiculturalism in the USA. In D. Bennett (ed) *Multicultural States: rethinking difference and identity.* London: Routledge

Goodson, I (2005) *Learning, Curriculum and Life Politics: the selected works of Ivor Goodson.* London: Routledge

Gonzalez, N, Moll, LC, Floyd-Tenery, M, Rivera, A, Rendon, P, Gonzales, R, Amanti, C (1993) *Teacher Research on Funds of Knowledge: learning from households.* National Center for Research on Cultural Diversity and Second Language Learning

Greig, A and Taylor, J (2002) *Doing Research with Children.* Sage: London

Gregory, E (1993) Sweet and sour: learning to read in British and Chinese schools. *English in Education* 27:3 53-59

Gregory, E (2001) Sisters and brothers as language and literacy teachers: synergy between siblings playing and working together. *Journal of Early Childhood Literacy* 1 (3) 301-322

Gregory, E (2008) *Learning to Read in a New Language.* London: Sage.

Gregory, E, Long, S and Volk, D (eds) (2004) *Many Pathways to Literacy: young children learning with siblings, grandparents, peers and communities.* London: Routledge

Gregory, E, Long, S and Volk, D (2004) Syncretic literacy studies: starting points. In E. Gregory, S. Long and D. Volk (eds) *Many Pathways to Literacy.* London: Routledge

Gregory, E and Williams A (2000) *City Literacies: learning to read across generations and cultures.* London: Routledge

Gussin Paley, V (1979) *White Teacher.* Cambridge, Mass: Harvard University Press

Hall, S (1990) Culture, identity and diaspora. In J. Rutherford (ed) *Identity, Community, Culture, Difference.* London: Lawrence and Wishart. 222-237

Hall, KA, Özerk, K, Zulfiqar, M and Tan, JEC (2002) 'This is Our School': provision, purpose and pedagogy of supplementary schooling in Leeds and Oslo. *British Educational Research Journal* 28(3) 399-418

Hammersley, M and Atkinson, P (1995) *Ethnography: Principles in Practice.* 2nd Edition. London: Routledge

Harris, R (2006) *New Ethnicities and Language Use.* Basingstoke: Palgrave/Macmillan

He, A (2000) Grammatical and sequential organization of teachers' directives. *Linguistics and Education.* 11(2) 119-140

He, A (2006) Toward an identity theory of the development of Chinese as a heritage language. *Heritage Language Journal* 4(1) 1-28

He, A (2008) An identity-based model for the development of Chinese as a heritage language. In A. He and Y. Xiao (eds) *Chinese as a Heritage Language: fostering rooted world citizenry.* Honolulu: University of Hawaii, National Foreign Language Resource Center

Heller, M (ed) (2007) *Bilingualism: a social approach.* Basingstoke: Palgrave/Macmillan

Heller, M (2007) Bilingualism as ideology and practice. In M. Heller (ed) *Bilingualism: a social approach.* Basingstoke: Palgrave Macmillan, 1-22

Heller, M (2006) *Linguistic Minorities and Modernity.* 2nd Edition. London: Continuum

Hermans, HJM and Kempen, HJG (1998) Moving cultures: the perilous problems of cultural dichotomies in a globalizing society. *American Psychologist* 22(10) 1111-1120

Hermans, HJM (2001a) The dialogical self: toward a theory of personal and cultural positioning. *Culture and Psychology* 7(3) 243-281

Hermans, HJM (2001b) Conceptions of self and identity: toward a dialogical view. *International Journal of Education and Religion* 2(1) 43-62

Hermans, HJM (2003) The construction and reconstruction of a dialogical self. *Journal of Constructivist Psychology* 16(2) 89-130

HMSO (2002) Race Relations (Amendment) Act 2002 http://www.culture.gov.uk/reference_library/publications/4794.aspx (last accessed 04/09)

Hornberger, N (2002) Multilingual language policies and the continua of biliteracy: an ecological approach. *Language Policy* (1) 27-51

Hornberger, N (2005) Opening and filling up implementational and ideological spaces in heritage language education. *The Modern Language Journal* 89(4) 605-609

Hornberger, N (2007) Multilingual language policies and the continua of biliteracy: an ecological approach. In O. Garcia and C.Baker, C (eds.) *Bilingual Education: an introductory reader.* Clevedon: Multilingual Matters 177-194

Hornberger, N and Wang, SC (2008) Who are our heritage language learners? Identity and biliteracy inheritage language education in the United States. In D. Brinton, O. Kagan, and S. Bauckus (eds.) *Heritage Language Education: a new field emerging.* New York/London: Routledge

House of Commons (2008) *Community Cohesion and Migration.* Communities and Local Government Committee – Tenth Report (HC 369-I), http://www.publications.parliament.uk/pa/cm200708/cmselect/cmcomloc/369/36902.htm (last accessed 01/09)

Irvine, J and Gal, S (2000) Language ideology and linguistic differentiation. In P. Kroskrity (ed) *Regimes of Language: ideologies, polities and identities*. Santa Fe/Oxford: School of American Research Press

Issa, T. (2008) Multiculturalism and inter-group dynamics: language, culture and identity of Turkish-speaking youth in the UK. In V. Lytra and J.N. Jørgensen (eds) *Multilingualism and Identities across Contexts: cross-disciplinary perspectives on Turkish-speaking youth in Europe*. Copenhagen Studies in Bilingualism 45

Issa, T. and Williams, C. (2009) *Realising Potential: complementary schools in the UK*. Stoke on Trent: Trentham

Jaffe, A (2007) Minority language movements. In M. Heller (ed) *Bilingualism: a social approach*. Basingstoke: Palgrave

Jia, G (2008) Heritage language development, maintenance, and attrition among recent Chinese immigrants in New York City. In A. He and Y. Xiao (eds) *Chinese as a Heritage Language: fostering rooted world citizenry*. Honolulu: University of Hawaii, National Foreign Language Resource Center

Jørgensen, JN and Quist, P (2007) Bilingual children in monolingual schools. In P. Auer and Li Wei (eds) *Handbook of Multilingualism and Multilingual Communication*. Berlin: Mouton de Gruyter

Kagan, O and Dillon, K (2008). Issues in heritage language learning in the United States. In N Van Deusen-Scholl and N Hornberger (eds) *Encyclopedia of Language and Education* 2nd Edition Vol. 4: Second and Foreign Language Education NY: Springer

Kaplan, C (1996) *Questions of Travel: postmodern discourses of displacement*. Durham, NC: Duke University Press

Kenner, C (2004a) Living in simultaneous worlds: difference and integration in bilingual script learning. *International Journal of Bilingual Education and Bilingualism* 7(1) 43-61

Kenner, C (2004b) Becoming biliterate: young children learning different writing systems. Stoke-on-Trent: Trentham Books

Kenner, C (2004c) Community school pupils reinterpret their knowledge of Chinese and Arabic for primary school peers. In E. Gregory, S. Long and Volk, D (eds) *Many Pathways to Literacy*. London: Routledge/Falmer.

Kenner, C, Gregory, E, Jessel, J, Arju, T, and Ruby, M (2004) *Intergenerational learning between children and grandparents in East London* (Final report, ESRC Project R000220131)

Kenner, C, Gregory, E and Ruby M (2007) *Developing bilingual learning strategies in mainstream and community contexts* (Final report, ESRC project R000221528)

Kenner, C, Ruby, M, Jessel, J, Gregory, E, and Arju, T (2008) Intergenerational learning events around the computer: a site for linguistic and cultural exchange. *Language and Education* 22 (4) 298-319

Kenner, C and Hickey, T (eds) (2008) *Multilingual Europe: diversity and learning*. Stoke-on-Trent: Trentham

Kijima, Y (2006) Caste and tribe inequality: Evidence from India, 1983-1999. *Economic Development and Cultural Change* 54 369-404

Kincheloe, J (2003) *Teachers as Researchers: qualitative inquiry as a path to empowerment*. London: Routledge/Falmer

Kirsch, C (2008) National Strategies on language in the European Context. In C. Kenner and T. Hickey (eds) *Multilingual Europe: diversity and learning*. Stoke-on-Trent: Trentham

Kraus, W (2000) Making identities talk. On qualitative methods in a longitudinal study [33 paragraphs] *Forum: Qualitative Social Research* 1(2) Art. 15http://nbn-resolving.de/urn:nbn:de:0114-fqs0002154 (last accessed 03/09)

Kress, G (1997) *Before Writing: rethinking the paths of literacy.* London: Routledge

Kress, G (2000) *Early Spelling: between convention and creativity.* London: Routledge

Kress, G and van Leeuwen, T (1996) *Reading Images: the grammar of visual design.* London: Routledge

Kress, G, Jewitt, C, Bourne, J, Franks, A, Hardcastle, J, Jones, K and Reid, E (2005) *English in Urban Classrooms: a multimodal perspective on teaching and learning.* London: Routledge

Li Wei (1994) *Three Generations Two Languages One Family: Language choice and language shift in the Chinese community in Britain.* Clevedon, Multilingual Matters

Li Wei (2006) Complementary schools, past, present and future. *Language and Education* 20(1) 76-83

Li Wei and Wu, C-J (2008) Code-switching: ideologies and practices. In A. He and Y. Xiao (eds) *Chinese as a Heritage Language: fostering rooted world citizenry.* Honolulu HI: National Foreign Language Resource Centre and University of Hawaii Press

Li Wei and Wu, C-J (2009) Polite Chinese children revisited: creativity and the use of code switching in the Chinese complementary school classroom. *International Journal of Bilingual Education and Bilingualism* 12(2) 193-211

Liao, Y (1992) The Chinese Community in Greater Manchester: The role of the catering trade. MPhil thesis: Manchester, University of Manchester

Luk, JCM (2008) Classroom discourse and the construction of learner and teacher identities. In M. Martin-Jones, A.M. de Mejia and N. Hornberger (eds) *Encyclopedia of Language and Education,* 2nd Edition, Volume 3: Discourse and Education 121-134

Lytle, J (1990) Reforming Urban Education: a review of recent reports and legislation. *The Urban Review* 22(3) p199-220

Lytra, V (forthcoming) Multilingualism and multimodality. In M. Martin-Jones, A. Blackledge and A. Creese (eds) *Handbook of Multilingualism.* London: Routledge

Lytra, V and Baraç, T with Creese, A, Bhatt, A, Blackledge, A, Hamid, S, Li Wei, Martin, P, Wu, C-J, and Yağcıoğlu-Ali, D (2008) Language practices, language ideologies and identity construction in London Turkish complementary schools. In V Lytra and JN Jørgensen (eds) *Multilingualism and Identities across Contexts: cross-disciplinary perspectives on Turkish-speaking youth in Europe.* Copenhagen Studies in Bilingualism. Volume 45

Lytra, V and Martin, P (2009) Rethinking complementary school classrooms: multilingual and multi-modal literacy practices, power and agency. Paper presented at the 3rd International Seminar on Language and Migration, AILA Language and Migration Network ReNLM, Universitat Autómoma de Barcelona, February 2-3, 2009

Martin, P, Bhatt, A, Bhojani, N and Creese, A (2006) Managing bilingual interaction in a Gujarati complementary school in Leicester. *Language and Education* 20(1) p5-22

Martin, P, Bhatt, A, Bhojani, B and Creese, A (2007) Multilingual learning stories in two Gujarati complementary schools in Leicester. In J. Conteh, P. Martin and L.H. Robertson (eds) *Multilingual Learning Stories in Schools and Communities in Britain.* Stoke-On-Trent: Trentham

Martin, P., Creese, A., Bhatt, A. and Bhojani, N (2004) *Complementary Schools and their Communities in Leicester* (final report). University of Leicester: ESRC R000223949. http://www.uel.ac.uk/education/staff/finalreport.pdf (06/09)

Martin-Jones, M and Saxena, M (1995) Supporting or containing bilingualism? Policies, power asymmetries and pedagogic practices in mainstream primary schools. In J. Tollefson (ed) *Power and Inequality in Language Education.* Cambridge: Cambridge University Press

Martin-Jones, M and Saxena, M (1996) Turn-taking, power asymmetries, and the positioning of bilingual participants in classroom discourse. *Linguistics and Education* 8 105-123

Mau, A, Francis, B and Archer, L (2009) Mapping politics and pedagogy: understanding the population and practices of Chinese complementary schools in England. *Ethnography in Education*, 4 (1) 17-36

May, S (2008) Bilingual/immersion education: what the research tells us. In J. Cummins and N. Hornberger (eds) *Encyclopedia of Language and Education.* 2nd Edition, Volume 5: Bilingual Education. NY: Springer

Maybin, J (2007) Literacy under and over the desk: Oppositions and heterogeneity. *Language and Education* 21(6): 515-530

McLaren, P and Torres, R (1999) Racism and multicultural education. In S May (ed) *Critical Multiculturalism.* London: Falmer Press

McPake, J, Tinsley, T and James, C (2007). Making provision for community languages: issues for teacher education in the UK. *Language Learning Journal* 35 (1) 99-112

Mehmet Ali, A (2001) *Turkish speaking Communities and Education: no delight.* London: Fatal Publications

Miller, J. (2003) *Audible Difference: ESL and social identity in schools.* Clevedon: Multilingual Matters.

Mills, J (2001) Being bilingual: perspectives of third generation Asian children on language, culture and identity. *International Journal of Bilingual Education and Bilingualism* 4(6) 383-402

Mirza, H and Reay, D (2000) Spaces and places of black educational desire: rethinking black supplementary schools as a new social movement. *Sociology* 345(3) p521-544

Moll, LC (2000) Inspired by Vygotsky: ethnographic experiments in education. In C.D. Lee and P. Smagorinsky (eds) *Vygotskian Perspectives on Literacy Research: constructing meaning through collaborative inquiry.* Cambridge: Cambridge University Press

Moll, L, Amanti, C, Neff, D and Gonzalez, N (1992) Funds of knowledge for teaching: using a qualitative approach to connect homes and classrooms. *Theory Into Practice* XXXI(2) 132-141

Moore, A (1999) *Teaching Multicultured Students.* London: Falmer

Moore, D (2002) Case Study: code-switching and learning in the classroom. *International Journal of Bilingual Education and Bilingualism* 5(5) 279-293

Norton, B (2000) *Identity and Language Learning: gender, ethnicity and educational change.* Harlow, Essex: Pearson Education

Ofsted (2007) *Gascoigne Primary School Inspection Report.* London: Ofsted

Osterman, K and Kottkamp, R (2004) *Reflective Practice for Educators.* 2nd Edition Thousand Oaks: Corwin Press

Pahl, K (2008) Language socialization and multimodality in multilingual urban homes. In P. A. Duff and N. Hornberger (eds) *Encyclopedia of Language and Education.* 2nd Edition, Volume 8: Language Socialization. NY: Springer

Pahl, K (in press) Interactions, intersections and improvisations: studying multimodal texts and classroom talk of six and seven year olds. *Journal of Early Childhood Studies*

Pahl, K. and Rowsell, J (2006) Introduction. In K. Palh. and J. Rowsell (eds.) *Travel Notes from the New Literacy Studies: instances of practice.* Clevedon: Multilingual Matters

Pantazi, E (2006) Teaching in Multicultural Societies: the theories and practice of teachers in Greek Community Schools. Unpublished PhD thesis, University of London

Pantazi, E (2008) Voices from the Greek community schools: bilingual pedagogy and teachers' theories. *Innovation in Language Learning and Teaching* 2 (2) pp189-205

Papapavlou, A and Pavlou, P (2001) The interplay of language use and language maintenance and the cultural identity of Greek Cypriots in the UK. *International Journal of Applied Linguistics* 11(1) 92-113

Parker, D (2000) The Chinese takeaway and the diasporic habitus. In: B. Hesse, *Un/settled Multi-culturalisms*. London: Zed Books

Patrick, D (2007) Language endangerment, language rights and indigeneity. In M. Heller (ed) *Bilingualism: a social approach*. Basingstoke: Palgrave

Paulston, CB (1977/1992) Language and Ethnic Boundaries. In Paulston CB (1992) *Sociolinguistic Perspectives on Bilingual Education*. Clevedon: Multilingual Matters

Pavlenko, A (2007) Autobiographic narratives as data in applied linguistics. *Applied Linguistics* 28(2) 163-188

Pavlenko, A and Blackledge, A (2004). New theoretical approaches to the study of negotiation of identities in multilingual contexts. In A. Pavlenko and A. Blackledge (eds) *Negotiation of Identities in Multilingual Contexts*. Clevedon: Multilingual Matters

Presidência do Conselho de Ministros (2008) Resolução do Conselho de Ministros n.º 188/2008, *Diário da República* – 1.ª Série, Nº 231, 27 de Novembro de 2008, 8525-8528. http://dre.pt/pdf1sdip/2008/11/23100/0852508528.pdf (last accessed 04/09 in Portuguese only)

Pujolar, J (2007) Bilingualism and the nation-state in the post-national era. In M. Heller (ed) *Bilingualism: a social approach*. Basingstoke: Palgrave

RAISE Project. *The Achievement of British Pakistani Learners*. www.insted.co.uk/raise.html (last accessed 30/07)

Rao, A (1999) The many sources of identity: an example of changing affiliations in rural Jammu and Kasmir. *Ethnic and Racial Studies* 22(1) 56-91

Rassool, N (1999) Flexible identities: exploring race and gender issues among a group of immigrant pupils in an inner – city comprehensive school. *British Journal of Sociology of Education* 20(1) 23-36

Reay, D and Mirza, H (1997) Uncovering genealogies of the margins: Black supplementary schooling. *British Journal of Sociology of Education* 18(4) 477-499

Ricento, T (2005). Problems with the 'language-as-resource' discourse in the promotion of heritage languages in the USA. *Journal of Sociolinguistics* 9(3) 348-368

Roberts, L (2000) Shifting Identities: an investigation into student and novice teachers' evolving professional identity. *Journal of Education for Teaching* 26(2) p184-186

Robertson, LH (2006) Learning to read 'properly' by moving between parallel literacy classes. *Language and Education* 20(1) 44-61

Robertson, LH (2007a) *The Role of Community Groups and Community Language Schools in Initial Teacher Education (ITE)* Report for Multiverse. http://www.multiverse.ac.uk/ViewArticle2.aspx?Keyword=leena+robertson&SearchOption=And&SearchType=Keyword&RefineExpand=1&ContentId=13101 (last accessed 04/09)

Robertson, LH (2007b) Bilingual children's story of learning to read. In J. Conteh, P. Martin and L.H. Robertson (eds) *Multilingual Learning Stories in Schools and Communities in Britain*. Stoke-on-Trent: Trentham

Rogoff, B (1990) *Apprenticeship in Thinking: cognitive development in social context*. New York: Oxford University Press

Rogoff, B. (2003) *The Cultural Nature of Human Development*. New York: Oxford University Press

Rogoff, B, Mosier, C, Mistry, J and Goncu, A (1993) Guided participation in cultural activity by toddlers and their caregivers. *Monographs of the Society for Research in Child Development,* 58 (8, Serial N. 236)

Rumberger, R and Larson K (1998) Toward explaining differences in educational achievement among Mexican American language-minority students. *Sociology of Education* 71 (January) 69-93

171

Schön, D (1983) *The Reflective Practitioner: how professionals think in action*. New York, Basic Books

Seddon, N, Cowen, N and Tree, O (2006) Supplementary schools: civil society strikes back. *CIVITAS Review* 3(4) http://www.civitas.org.uk/pdf/CivitasReviewDecember06.pdf (last accessed 01/09)

Sikes, P, Measor, L, and Woods, P (2001) Critical phases and incidents. In J. Soler, A. Craft and H Burgess (eds) *Teacher Development: exploring our own practice*. London: Paul Chapman Publishing

Singh, G (2003) Multiculturalism in contemporary Britain: reflections on the Leicester model. *International Journal on Multicultural Societies* 5(1) 40-54

Sneddon, R (1997) Working towards partnership: parents, teachers and community organisations. In J. Bastiani (ed) *Home-School work in Multicultural Settings*. London: David Fulton

Sneddon, R (2007) Learning in three languages in home and community. In J. Conteh, P. Martin, P and L.H. Robertson (eds) *Multilingual Learning Stories from Schools and Communities in Britain*. Stoke-On-Trent: Trentham

Sneddon, R (2008) Magda and Albana: learning to read with dual language books. *Language and Education* 22 (2) p137-154

Sneddon, R (2009) *Bilingual Books, Biliterate Children: learning to read through dual language books*, Stoke-on-Trent: Trentham

Sneddon, R and Martin, P (2008) Creating spaces for maintaining/developing languages, literacies and identities in East London. Paper presented at the Association Internationale de Linguistique Appliquée Conference. Essen, 24-29 August 2008

Soin, H and Flynn, M (2005) Emotion and rhythm in critical incidents learning. *Interchange* 36(1-2) 73-83

Song, M. (2009) Is intermarriage a good indicator of integration? *Journal of Ethnic and Migrant Studies*, 35 (2) 331-348

Souza, ABB (2006) Should I speak Portuguese or English? Ethnic and social identity construction in the language choices of Brazilian mothers and their mixed-heritage children at home and in a community language school in the UK. Unpublished PhD thesis, University of Southampton

Souza, A (2008) How linguistic and cultural Identities are affected by migration Language Issues *NATECLA* 19(1) 36-42

Stone, R, Muir, H and Smith, L (2004) *Islamophobia: issues, challenges and action*. A Report by the Commission on British Muslims and Islamophobia. Stoke-on-Trent: Trentham

Stone, CA (1993) What is missing in the metaphor of scaffolding? In A. Forman, N. Minick and C.A. Stone (eds) *Contexts for Learning: sociocultural dynamics in children's development*. New York: Oxford University Press

Street, B. (ed) (1993) *Cross-cultural Approaches to Literacy*. Cambridge: Cambridge University Press

Taylor, MJ (1987) *Chinese Pupils in Britain: A Review of Research into the Education of Pupils of Chinese Origin*. Windsor: NFER-NELSON

Thomas, WP and Collier, V (2002) *A National Study of School Effectiveness for Language Minority Students' Long-Term Academic Achievement*. Center for Research on Education, Diversity and Excellence (CREDE). Berkeley, Graduate School of Education University of California. http://crede.

Training and Development Agency for Schools (TDA) (2007) *Professional Standards for Teachers*. London: TDA http://www.tda.gov.uk/teachers/professionalstandards/standards.aspx (last accessed 12/08)

Training and Development Agency for Schools (TDA) (undated) *Community access*. http://www. tda.gov.uk/remodelling/extendedschools/whatarees/communityaccess.aspx (last accessed 01/09)

 berkeley.edu/research/llaa/1.1_final.html (last accessed 01/09)

Tripp, D (1993) *Critical Incidents in Teaching*. London: Routledge

Tsow, M (1980) Chinese children and multi-cultural education. *Education Journal* 2(2) 6

Tsow, M (1983) Analysis of responses to a national survey on mother tongue teaching in local education authorities 1980-1982. *Educational Research* 25(3) 202-208

Valdés, G, Gonzalez, S, Garcia, DL, and Marquez, P (2008) Heritage languages and ideologies of language: unexamined challenges. In D Brinton, O Kagan, and S Bauckus (eds) *Heritage Language Education: a new field emerging*. New York/London: Routledge

Valsiner, J (2000) *Culture and Human Development*. London: Sage Publications

Valsiner, J (2004) Temporal integration of structures within the dialogical self. Paper presented at the Third International Conference on the Dialogical Self. Warsaw, Poland

Verma, G, Chan, Y, Bagley, C, Sham, S, Darby, D, Woodrow, D and Skinner, G (1999) *Chinese Adolescents in Britain and Hong Kong*. Aldershot: Ashgate

Vygotsky, L S (1978) *Mind in Society: the development of higher psychological processes*. Cambridge, MA: Harvard University Press

Wang, X (1996) Introduction. In: X. Wang (ed) *A View from Within: A case study of Chinese heritage community language schools in the United States*. Washington DC: National Foreign Language Center

Wells, G (2001) Learning to pay attention to other modes of meaning making. In G. Wells (ed) *Action, Talk and Text*. New York: Teachers' College Press

Williams, C (1996) Secondary education: teaching in the bilingual situation. In C Williams, G Lewis and C Baker (eds) *The Language Policy: Taking stock*. Llangefni: CAI.

Williams, M (2002) Generalisation in interpretative research. In T. May (ed) *Qualitative Research in Action*. London: Sage

Wood, D, Bruner, J and Ross, G (1976) The role of tutoring in problem solving. *Journal of Child Psychology* 17 89-100

Wu, C-J (2001) Learning Cultures: The example of learning Chinese as community language in Chinese schools in the UK. Unpublished PhD thesis. Leicester: University of Leicester

Wu, C-J (2006) Look who's talking: Language choices and culture of learning in UK Chinese classrooms. *Language and Education* 20(1) 62-75

You, H (2006) *The Chinese Community in UK 2006*. London: Mei and Ken Co. Ltd

Zhou, M and Kim, S (2006) Community forces, social capital and educational achievement: the case of supplementary education in the Chinese and Korean communities. *Harvard Educational Review,* Spring edition, 1-29

Zhou, M and Li, X-Y (2003) Ethnic language schools and the development of supplementary education in the immigrant Chinese community in the United States. *New Directions for Youth Development,* Winter, 57-73

# Index